# Medicine of the Cherokee

# Medicine
## of the
# Cherokee

## *The Way of*
## *Right Relationship*

J.T. Garrett, Ed.D., M.P.H,

and Michael Tlanusta Garrett, Ph. D.

Eastern Band of Cherokee

BEAR & COMPANY
PUBLISHING
ROCHESTER, VERMONT

LIBRARY OF CONGRESS CATALOGING-IN-PUBLICATION DATA

Garrett, J. T., 1942-
   Medicine of the Cherokee : the way of right relationship / J. T. Garrett
and Michael T. Garrett.
      p. cm.
   ISBN 1-879181-37-1
   1. Cherokee Indians—Medicine.     2. Cherokee Indians—Religion.
3. Indians of North America—Medicine.   I. Garrett, Michael T., 1970- .
II. Title
E99. C5G237  1996
615. 8' 82' 089975—dc20                                                    96-16156
                                                                              CIP

Bear & Company, Inc.
Rochester, Vermont
Bear & Company is a division of Inner Traditions International
www.InnerTraditions.com

Cover and interior design: Melinda Belter
Cover illustration: Francene Hart
Text illustrations: Debi Duke
Editing: Gerry Clow and Sonya Moore
Printed in the United States

20  19  18  17  16  15  14  13  12  11  10  9  8

*Lovingly dedicated to those who have walked before us, and those yet to come. Together, we are all dancing the Sacred Dance.*

# Contents

# Preface & Acknowledgments

*"Medicine is a way of life, an object or ceremony having power or control over influences that may affect a person, and a path toward restoring health.*

—FROM THE TEXT

A small boy searches for a way to explain life with all its complexities. His Cherokee grandfather smiles and explains life in all its simplicities.

Many years later, another small boy talks about the simple things of life, while his father describes how complex life is today. Inside, the father feels the not-so-distant words of his grandfather speaking softly:

> You are not just alive, you are part of all life itself. You are kin to all things, and everything has life . . . and memory.

Things have a way of coming full circle—as a way of completing the Circle, and creating opportunities for life, love, growth, feeling, and learning. The wisdom of the past becomes the bridge to the future, like the rising and setting of the Sun in a continuous motion of ageless beauty. Healing becomes the understanding of a calm spirit, connecting the memory of our ancestors and all living things, experiencing a sense of oneness in the energy-flow of choice and presence through unity of mind, body, spirit, and natural environment.

This is the wisdom of the Cherokee, and of many tribes or cultures of people all over the world. It is more than knowledge. It is more than understanding that comes from reading a book. It is an experience that flows from one day to the next for a spirit among all living beings, from one generation to the next.

This book represents many of the old stories and teachings, which have been offered for the purpose of guiding us in our life-journey to becoming better "helpers" for the protection of Mother Earth and all our relatives. We feel very proud to be able to bring some of this wisdom to those interested and willing to seek out and honor their own vision as we all walk our individual paths. We may come from many different tribes, but we are all of one family.

A very special thanks goes to many Cherokee Elders who have been willing to share for the benefit of others. All of our Elders are very special and are to be honored as beloved people for living and sharing their experiences. A heartfelt thanks goes to family and friends who have supported, nurtured, protected, and, in some cases, tolerated us along the way.

We thank Barbara and Gerry Clow, our editors at Bear & Company, for their openness and persistence throughout the process of getting this book to publication. We especially thank Debi Duke for the illustrations that moved our spirits by capturing our thoughts and the theme of harmony and balance. We thank the many friends and others who encouraged us to follow our vision for this book.

We thank a very special wife and mother, Phyllis, lovingly referred to as "Mama Bear," for her loving patience, humor, strength, and sense of compassion. We thank a very special mother and grandmother, Ruth Rogers Garrett, and her sister, Shirley Arch, for sharing their stories and their understanding of Nature. "Mama" Garrett dedicated her life to family and friends, as an example of being a Cherokee woman and "helper" to everyone she ever met.

We thank a very special daughter and sister, Melissa, for showing us that all of us have our own "Medicine," as well as our own lessons, challenges, and means of healing.

Last, but not least, thanks goes to you, the reader, for continuing, renewing, or beginning this new journey for the sake of yourself and all those with whom you are connected. May you walk the path of Good Medicine in harmony and balance. Together, we come full circle in the Medicine of the Cherokee, living the way of right relationship. "Wah Doh."

# MEDICINE OF THE CHEROKEE

# PART ONE

# THE INDIAN MEDICINE STORY:

## A Cherokee Perspective

by

J. T. Garrett

# Keepers of the Secrets

**M**y grandfather and I were sitting on a large rock on the edge of the Oconaluftee River on a warm spring day. I was looking into a small pool of water that was caught in an etched indentation of a rock. There were small minnows moving around. My grandfather said, "What do you see?" I was very young and he seemed tall, even sitting down. "I see the little fish swimming around, but they have no place to go." "Are you afraid for them or yourself?" My grandfather would often ask two questions at once. "The sun is hot, and I am afraid they will get too hot in the shallow water, besides, what if they don't get back to their parents in the river?" I often didn't answer the questions asked, but used it as a chance to say what else I was thinking about. "Well, maybe they are alright in this special little pool of water. They might get out into the large river and a larger fish come by and eat them for dinner." Wow, I hadn't thought of that. "What will they eat to stay alive and what if they stay there and grow too big for the little pool of water?"

I guess I must have learned to ask two questions as well from my grandfather.

"Grandson," he said, "you do not need to worry because Nature will take care of them. Whatever happens is all part of a greater plan of life. It is the Great One's plan. There are things you cannot see with your eyes that the minnows feed upon and there are larger fish that will feed upon them. The 'little fish' as you call them must learn to hide in the plants until they are strong enough to move quicker than the bigger fish. They will grow smart and outsmart the bigger fish whose belly is too full from its own greed. Life is like that." Grandfather told me much more that afternoon, but somehow, I can only remember about the little fish. That was the lesson of the little fish. There were not many more stories to be told by my grandfather to share with me, because he did not live long after that. I do cherish those special moments. Little did I realize that he was one of the keepers of the secrets. He understood about life and the story of Indian Medicine. Knowing that he would not be able to share with me for much longer, he made sure that I would learn the Medicine Way from other Medicine Men and Women (whom I'll refer to as Medicine Elders from now on).

This story of Indian Medicine begins with the many stories that were shared by many elder Native American teachers. There is a simple innocence about the complex nature of Nature. As a Nachez Medicine Elder once said to me, "It (Nature) is as it always was, but we as humans try to change it to make it ours. In fact, we are the younger, 'cause Nature was here before us. So we must honor Nature, and in doing so, we honor our ancestors who realized the critical balance we have with all things." This chapter is about my

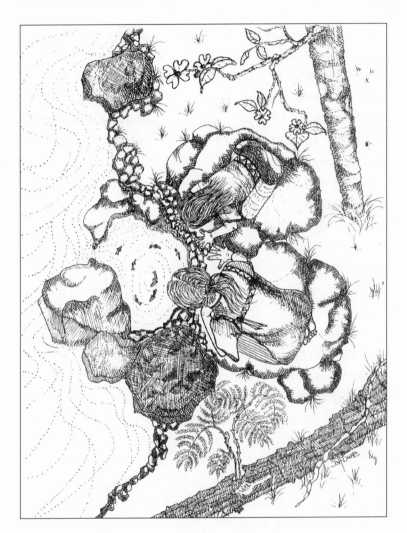

experience and training in Indian Medicine with the keepers of the secrets. I feel very proud to be the one chosen to tell this story.

Reference is made in this book to "Elders," who are Grandfathers and Grandmothers. This is an honorable title given to those who are respected in my tribe and in other

American Indian and Alaska Native tribes (that I will refer to in the rest of the book as simply "Native American tribes" or "Native Americans"). It is an honor earned with time, experience, and in helping others. The term "Medicine" as used with "Medicine Elder" is a reference to a Medicine Man or Woman. I am a member of the Eastern Band of Cherokee Indians from the mountains of North Carolina. At the age of 52, I was told by the Medicine Elders it was alright for me to tell this story. It was my vision as a student of Indian Medicine to share so that anyone interested would better appreciate Indian Medicine as more than an archaic herbal way. The natural way and healing by self-choices promoted by Indian Medicine are included in almost every "alternative" therapy today. With a blend of stories and teachings, I want to share what I was taught about the beginning of Indian Medicine.

It was my father who encouraged me to learn the Medicine. He was a wonderful and protective Irishman of several generations in America. His family brought a wealth of knowledge and skills in folk medicine for survival. Mixing with the Cherokee in western North Carolina, they survived well in the mountains. As my mother would share stories from a Cherokee perspective, my father had similar stories from Irish mythology and his own experiences growing up near the Eastern Cherokee Indian Reservation. It was from this background that I realized that there are many similarities in cultures and stories of people all over the world. My intent was to promote a better understanding, while protecting the sacred aspects of the Native American culture, and sharing the "Good Medicine Way" or Cherokee traditional teachings. The purpose of Good Medicine is to bring about peace and healing through harmony and balance. This was needed in the beginning of time, and it is needed even more so today. Ironically, it was my father who had lost the Irish teachings that helped me to realize why I really needed to learn and share the Medicine Way when the time was right.

The problems and concerns we face today are staggering, with the environmental stress and pollution, crime and violence, and other negative influences that harm us today. In an earlier time in America, conservation and revitalization of Mother Earth were of utmost concern because we had to live off the land, and the keepers of the secrets were helpers to us in that regard. These were farmers, loggers, hunters, herb doctors, mothers, uncles, grandmothers, and grandfathers who shared with each other the secrets learned, to help each other. Many did not have a certificate or a degree. They have just always been here when we needed help. As one Elder said, "We have been so busy learning and doing, that we have forgotten how to really listen." This book is also about us spiraling to a higher level of awareness and understanding based upon the "spirit-learning," as one Elder called it. This is within each of us, as a memory from many genes and many generations since the beginning of time. This book is about finding something special in our lives that Native Americans call Good Medicine.

. . . . . . . . . . . . . . . . . . . . . . . . . . . . . . . . . . . . . . . . . . . . . . . . . .

## FINDING SOMETHING SPECIAL

Do you remember finding something in Nature and saving it in a special box or place? Maybe it was a rock, a bird feather, a crystal, or even an acorn. You just had to put it in a special place. My first Medicine Bag—using the term "Medicine" in the Native American way—was magical, sacred, and special for me. Of course, there was probably something in your special place or written in your diary that you did not want others to know. It was personal and private to you. Well, Indian Medicine is that way for Native Americans, as well as for many other tribes and indigenous peoples from islands and isolated locations in the world. In this book, the sharing will be with the understanding that specific sacred things and ceremonies will not be revealed, but respected as being sacred to an individual tribe. There is more than enough that can be shared that can guide us in finding something special.

My mother, Ruth Rogers Garrett, taught me many Cherokee stories. She taught through example to be a helper to everyone you ever meet. She taught me that everyone is special in this life, that love has no boundaries, and that boundaries cannot be set on love. She still has rhymes and songs that she shares with us. I still have a strong image of her in our small flower garden working and even talking with the herbs and plants. My first lessons were to respect all life, protect Mother Earth, and nurture the plants and herbs. I look whenever I go home to the Reservation to see if comfrey, fennel, catnip, rosemary, and many of the plants that we care for are still growing in the backyard. Sure enough, they are always there, reminding me that life does go on. Aunt Shirley would tell me stories of the Spirit People and teach me how to "mix Medicine" from Nature's gifts. She knew how to survive and knew the lessons of the animals. My Grandfather Oscar Rogers learned as a young Cherokee how to track animals, eat food from the wild, and recognize plants and herbs from arrowwood to yellowwood. Even my great grandmother was an herb doctor in the Tennessee mountains, or "hills" as they called them. Aunt Shirley learned, along with others in my family, how to survive. While she and my mother did not have the degrees in herbology, they were the best teachers about herbs that a young person could have around. I was truly blessed. And they too were some of the keepers of the secrets.

In my youth on the Cherokee Reservation in North Carolina, my Medicine Bag took on a new significance as I began to study Indian Medicine. My vision was sharing some of the teachings and "bridging the gap," a term I will explain later in this book. My Medicine Bag continues to change with new things replacing old things and vice versa, with the realization that Indian Medicine is dynamic and continues to change, as opposed to some things that will always stay the same. As a Medicine Elder said, "Your Medicine is your life, and your life is represented by all those things that you have said, that have been given to you, and that you have given others, and it is all that you are. Your Medicine is all the things that you 'bundle' together in the form of objects that you hold sacred to the world." I came to realize that Medicine, unlike the term "medicine," is not just a substance used in the treatment of disease or an agent used to restore health as taught in the dictionary. The Elder said, "If you believe only what you read to be true, then you will miss the greatest part of your Medicine, 'cause you will limit yourself to just what you see. There is much more to life than what meets the eye." The dynamics of the lessons taught by Native American Elders remind us that not all understanding is in the books. There is still much to learn and relearn in life's lessons.

The Elder went on to explain that Medicine is a way of life, an object or ceremony having power or control over

influences that may affect a person, and a path toward restoring health. Medicine usually includes more than the individual; it often includes the family, clan, and tribe in a natural or
universal setting. Each person's Medicine is sacred and powerful among Native Americans, as it is for everybody. By
learning more about our ancient and traditional or cultural
teachings, we can "bridge the gap" in our own lives for a
more healthful and balanced life.

...............................................................

### A CHEROKEE STORY: THE BOYS

Early Indian stories are ways to communicate values
and lessons that remain dynamic, whether one thousand
years ago or one thousand years ahead. The stories are a part
of our "Medicine" for values, direction, and healing. Many
stories are used in this book for you to better appreciate
bridging-the-gap in your own life. Some Elders say the
Cherokee originated from a place far away, possibly even
from the stars and the "star spirits." There is a story, long
guarded as the origin of the use of pine in ceremonies and at
certain special times for burning to carry a message to the
stars. As the story goes, very early in our existence, there were
seven boys who used to do almost nothing but play the
Indian ball game of using a stick to move a round stone
across the ground. Their mothers were not pleased because
the boys would not work in the cornfield. Once they were
very hungry after playing ball, and they went home to eat.
Their mothers put the ball stones in water and said, "Since
you won't work, you can have the stones instead of corn for
your supper."

The young boys were upset, and they went away saying,

"We will never come back home again." They were doing the Feather Dance, which was to dance using small steps around in a circle, praying to the spirits to take them away. Suddenly, their feet were lifting off the ground as they continued to dance around and around. The mothers went to find the boys and noticed that they were going higher and higher upward toward the great skyvault. The mothers tried to pull them down, but they kept going upward. One mother hung on to her son, and he suddenly fell to the ground with a thunder. The other six were suddenly pulled higher and higher until they went into the skyvault.

Some say that we now see them at night as the Pleiades or "The Boys," as they are called by the Cherokee. The seventh boy who struck the ground fell so hard that he was covered by the earth, never to be found again. The mothers grieved every day, shedding tears on the ground where the boys once were. One day they noticed that a small tree started to sprout from the spot where the seventh boy struck the ground. Today that tree is known as the Pine That Grows Very Tall, trying to reach his friends, The Boys, in the skyvault. The pine is considered sacred and used in some ceremonies and burials. It is also said that if you listen to certain pine trees when the wind blows, you will hear messages from the spirits of The Boys.

Early Cherokee stories, and those of other Native Americans, sometimes refer to star spirits and how they influence our lives. The energy of light from the Sun, the Moon, and all the stars is considered by elder teachers as connected strongly to us. The stars had a special significance to those who looked up into the skyvault at the brilliance and magical power of the lights that would sometimes move about in the heavens. Unlike the daytime when the sky would have the Sun or clouds, the sky at night was active with "star spirits" or "star people." It is easy to understand why many of the earlier stories originated from gazing at the wonder and power of stars that would even move on occasion in the huge sky above. They also say that is the reason why we are connected to the stars, energies, and cycles of the great sky-vault above us.

Native Americans understood the delicate and critical balance of Mother Earth with the Universal Circle. The balance of the environment was emphasized in the stories and the teachings as sacred values. This same balance is what we call homeostasis in our bodies, which must be in balance with the Universal Circle as well. If Earth experiences an earthquake, it affects us too. Every harm to Mother Earth is also harm to us, our well being and our health. This is the reason that Native Americans show respect in ceremonies, dances, and song-chants to the Four Directions, the Upper World, and the Lower World. We learn to understand the critical balance of our lives with Mother Earth as a physical, mental, spiritual, and natural connection.

• • • • • • • • • • • • • • • • • • • • • • • • • • • • • • • • • • • • • • • • • • •

## A TIME FOR SHARING

As Indian people, we were taught that sacred things were not to be shared, except among our own tribes. According to some Native American Elders, it was alright for me to share some of the stories and sacred things, particularly after a vision I received in 1987, but only to create peace and understanding in the world. My vision quest that year involved seeing a large white eagle flying over the Great

Smoky Mountains; somehow I knew it was time for us as people to relearn the ancient teachings for regaining harmony and balance. As one Elder put it, "We have learned too much today, so much that we have forgotten how to learn the important lessons of life. We think we 'gotta' learn everything from a book. The truth is that we had better learn the truths, those taught by the Ancient Ones." During the same year, the American Indian Religious Freedom Act was passed under President Carter. This piece of legislation provided protection from earlier persecution about sacred beliefs, activities, and places honored by Native Americans. Most of what has been shared with the public about Indian stories of life is through sketchy myths recorded by mostly nonIndian writers, researchers, and anthropologists. Language differences and perceptions affected how these stories and teachings were told and understood. However, there is a story to tell, by the Indian keepers of the secrets, as only they could have told it in a traditional and cultural way.

......................................................

## IN THE BEGINNING

The Cherokee story spoke of the origins of life itself. It told of spirit people in the skyvault coming to Mother Earth and the beginning of the First Fire. As the story goes, the universe was like a giant sea of water flowing freely as a huge pool of energy with no physical form. As one Medicine Elder put it, "Scientists and those others who 'think they know' are on the right track, but they often look at the little things and say, 'I wonder how this came to be?' instead of looking at the whole and the little things as pieces of the larger puzzle of life."

As the story goes, Mother Earth is suspended at the Sacred Four Directions by a twine of energy from the sky-vault, which is solid like a rock, but we just cannot see it. Each of us, being held in suspension by the same Four Directions, consists of energy as a child of Father Sun and Mother Earth. This delicate existence is considered to be under our care. If we do not protect Mother Earth, she will drop her energy cords at each of the Four Directions and plunge down into the sea of infinity. Therefore, Native Americans have always understood themselves to be the keepers of Mother Earth, as good children protecting the elder parents.

In recent years, a worldwide environmental movement has focused on protecting Earth from pollutants and hazardous energy and dangerous radiation. We are concerned about Mother Earth and the adverse effect that our existence has had on her. She has a tremendous ability to continuously revive and "clear" herself. This has been the case in many renewed beginnings of humankind after disasters over millions of years. A real question in the minds of many people today is whether Earth will survive the many generations to come who may not understand the delicate balance of our existence with the star spirits in the sky. The stories and the wisdom of the Native American ancestors are not to be taken lightly. These teachings focus on values learned from millions of years of survival. As an Elder put it, "We are at the end of a beginning and at the beginning again; it is a matter of what we want to do with our choices." Native American teachings show that we are the chosen "animal" with choices, and Good Medicine choices must be made to maintain the harmony and balance of Mother Earth. Some feel that we must make these critical choices within the next seven years.

These are the critical years, according to the keepers of the secrets, as we spiral to a new plane of spiritual existence with a renewed understanding. As an Elder said, "We must go back to the beginning to understand that there is an end and a new beginning to everything!" The secret is Good Medicine choices for harmony and balance.

..........................................................

## THE CHEROKEE STORY OF THE BEGINNING OF MOTHER EARTH

This story has been told many times, but I want to tell it as it was told to me. In another time, the Cherokee Spirit People were in the skyvault. It was getting crowded in the skyvault, and the Great One decided it was time for spirit beings to become physical beings and spread out of the skyvault. There was a Great Council meeting of all the spirit beings to decide on the plan. The Great One said, "Those of you who choose to be a part of the creation of Mother Earth will also have to protect her. The Cherokee Spirit People have been chosen to be keepers of the secrets and keepers of Mother Earth and all living things that go over into the physical world. They will be given the power Medicine of choice to do this. Other human spirits of tribes will also follow, and they will be given the power Medicine of choice to be keepers as well."

Earth at that time was like a large island floating in a sea and held in place by four Cords of Life. The Great One said, "These 'Cords of Life' will hold Mother Earth suspended as long as everything is held in sacred balance. These spirit beings will include the four-legged ones, the two-legged ones, the many-legged ones, the no-legged ones, and the winged ones. Everything and everyone will live in harmony, interdependent on one another for sustained life and regeneration of life."

It was the first task of the Animal Clan to go down to learn what they could about this new Earth. The little Water Beetle of the Beaver's grandchild went first, fluttering around, but it could not find a place to land. Soon it dropped into the water many times, coming up with muddy feet, and that mud became islands. The Bird Clan said it wanted to go down because they could fly for long distances to search for a place to land. The Great Buzzard flew down, but he was so large that he tired quickly, and his large wings kept striking the water and churning up mud that made mountains and valleys until he returned home in the skyvault.

By this time, Earth was dry where the Animal Clan and the Bird Clan stirred the mud from the water as the Sun tracked across. The Fish Clan said they wanted to go down into the water and just stay there, but some wanted to be able to walk on the land. What we now call the Crawfish did crawl up on the red clay, and he was baked in the hot sun, so that today we call him the Red Crawfish. On the seventh day, some of the Animal Clan, who were hiding in the mud because of the hot sun, came up to take a look. The first of these was the worm, and he was burned so badly that we call him the Red Worm. It was still hot, and they called to the Great One for help.

The Great One came down on the seventh day, hearing the prayers, and brought many beautiful plants and trees to provide the air for the Cherokee to breath into their lungs and become physical human beings. Of course, they were not used to breathing, so they had to rest that first day, but they would work for six days and learn to rest at night when the Sun would rest. The Great One was very proud of the spirit beings for the good work they had done. He asked the Thunder Beings to strike a tree so the fragile physical beings would have heat from the Sacred Fire. From that time on, all the animal, insect, bird, tree, plant, and human clans would give ceremony around the fire and dance for the Sun to celebrate and honor the gift of life on a now-living Mother Earth.

........................................................

## MODERN-DAY SECRETS

There are many secrets that affect our health and medicine today. From the Medicine of Native Americans to the modern medicine, there will always be keepers coming forward with reality options and stories of wellness and miracle cures from new discoveries. In the United States today, there exist some of the finest and most modern medical treatments in the world. We are truly gifted. While some Americans may feel frustrated with a lack of success in treating cancer, AIDS, and some other diseases, we are much healthier than our forefathers in many ways. Many of us, for example, can choose homeopathy or naturopathy, therapies that allow complementary allopathic and osteopathic treatments. It has been my experience that we truly have choices in medical care that we can add to our Medicine Bag.

The real challenge for health-care professionals and medical-care professionals is to allow and promote healing and prevention. Those choices include many alternative therapies that will be the integral therapies of tomorrow. **Ayurveda,** for example, is a preventive medicine based on a 5000-year-old system of treating and preventing disease with a focus on physical, emotional, spiritual, and mental traits of a person. As with Indian Medicine, the approach is focused on balance by keeping life forces flowing freely. The treatment modality is based on a balance of life activities.

There are many therapies today that are similiar to Indian Medicine. These examples of present-day therapies today are the secrets of yesterday: **herbal medicine** that uses botanical medicines as remedies or treatments for ailments or illness; **chiropractic** with manipulation of the musculoskeletal structures of the body for a proper relationship with the nervous system; **hydrotherapy** using water, "sweats" or saunas, and steam treatments; **guided imagery** with concentration on specific, directed, mental images for relaxation and for boosting the immune system to combat disease; **Feldenkrais Method** for movement exercises designed to release habitual patterns of tension related to posture and movement; **therapeutic massage** with systematic application of pressures to muscles to promote relaxation and increase circulation; **shiatsu** as acupressure on points of the body for improving energy flow and balance, similar to acupuncture; **Rolfing** using the thumbs and other appendages to manipulate connective tissue for proper alignment of the body; **qigong** as a system of exercise with a focus on breathing, meditation, and movement to restore the flow of vital energy and to boost natural healing; **t'ai chi chuan** as a form of meditation with movement and slow-motion exercises with coordinated breathing for improving energy flow in the body and spirit; and many more, such as **hypnotherapy** with an induced state of influence, **magnetic field therapy** with the use of magnets to stimulate or calm pain and to promote the body's natural healing, and **meditation** to quiet the mind and focus on calm, control, and receiving the gift of healing. These gifts are all parts of our Good Medicine Way that is with us today.

A special therapy that has been around for over 100 years with values similar to Indian Medicine is **homeopathy**. The symptoms of the body are related to its natural defenses, and the small amounts of remedies are to provoke a specific response. This is referred to as the Law of Similars. As in Indian Medicine, homeopathy teaches that the highly diluted drugs are more potent than the concentrated drugs, called the Law of Infinitesimals. The illness and its remedy is specifically suited to the person, based on a profile that includes the physical, emotional, and mental states in the total-symptom picture. This seems very effective in treating chronic arthritis, headaches, autoimmune diseases, and allergies, as well as many acute infections. The thing I like is the home-care approach with self-care manuals.

**Naturopathy** traces its roots back to the approaches used by my great grandmother who emphasized prevention and use of combinations of remedies that act as "helpers" for the body's natural healing power. This is very similar to Indian Medicine. The modern training for a naturopath includes a standard medical workup with training in traditional Chinese medicine and Ayurvedic medicine, including herbal medicine, acupuncture, hydrotherapy, massage, therapeutic exercise, and counseling. Many of the secrets of commonsense approach to health and medical care are available in this therapy.

Other secrets that have become more popular today include **orthomolecular nutritional medicine**. By adjusting the balance of vitamins, minerals, amino acids, and other nutrients in the body, the focus is on the patient participating in well-being, rather than on the illness. Similarly, Indian Medicine focuses on the balance and adjustments in life with remedies to bring about harmony. Orthomolecular physicians, like osteopathic and allopathic physicians, can treat a broad range of acute and chronic diseases that also include psychiatric illnesses. **Chinese medicine** focuses on prevention, using the secret of detecting energy flow in the body to find the illness or problem before it happens or manifests in the body. Similarly, Indian Medicine focuses on detecting and clarifying choices that a person can make to prevent illness and disruption of the harmony and balance. While other therapies will be mentioned in this book, there are many secrets from the keepers of the secrets that have emerged in many alternative and complementary therapies that are available today. As the Medicine Elders say, "We are the human spirit beings who have choice, but we must find it for ourselves." We can do that by seeking the secrets of the keepers who have been given the gift of understanding.

......................................................

### THE SECRETS OF THE KEEPERS

As a student of Indian Medicine, I ran into difficulty when someone would criticize me or one of my elder teachers. It was also difficult for me to live the traditional Medicine, then put on the suit and tie and be a hospital administrator in the white man's way. My first mistake was to present myself the way I was *told* to do. It broke the Native American way of presenting myself as a helper. I overheard a tribal member say, "He is going to be like the rest," and I knew that she was talking about *control*. The Native

American person accepts you as you want to be. However, they respect you for how you are with others. Humility and the Rule of Acceptance helped me to cope with criticisms. They also helped me to better appreciate the unique values and teachings of Indian Medicine. One of the important lessons for me to learn was having the negative energy move around me, instead of internalizing and reacting to criticisms. The Rule of Acceptance is the ability to accept anything said or done with the realization that it is what another says or does, not what we say or do. In this case, an action does not necessarily require a reaction, but an *interaction*. This interaction may be with the person or persons creating the action, or it can be with someone else to clarify or resolve a state of nonacceptance. As a student and apprentice, I was to accept everything and learn to listen. This can be very difficult in an environment where we are taught to be assertive, to analyze, critique, and "take charge." There were many more lessons to learn in Indian Medicine and in life.

On one occasion, I became angry at a person who strongly criticized my Medicine Elder for including her spiritual beliefs in using herbs. He got to the point of yelling at her, and I retaliated, so to speak, causing harm to the other person. My teacher would not speak to me for over four days. When she spoke, her words were strong: "You were chosen, not by yourself or by any human being, but by a power better than you and me. Don't listen to those who would criticize you or me for being in the Medicine. Live the truth of the Native American ancestors, and I will tell you, they would have forgiven the person. Instead, you gave your power away!"

It was apparent to me that she was not pleased because

I was not to interfere with her lesson, nor to make a new one for myself. The idea of giving my power away was a thought, and a lesson that I was to go up on the mountain and learn by myself. I realized that I did not "turn the other cheek," but how was I supposed to just sit there and listen? It suddenly dawned on me that just because someone stands there and yells, this does not mean that I have to stand there and listen. I learned the lesson of acceptance. The spiritual power entrusted in me was more important than the person trying to take the power away from me. I learned something about the lesson of the opposites, and was able to look at things both ways and in the third person. The Elder said, as I returned that evening, "It is time for all of us to evolve to a higher level of understanding about these things, in a spiritual way. Find ways to understand the fears that others face. They wear a mask, you don't have to, unless you have something to hide. If that is the case, then you don't need to be in the Medicine yet! If you are going to defend someone, let it be those who need us, such as the four-legged and the winged ones who are disappearing, or defend our Earth Mother from the pollution and destruction, and defend the little spirit ones (under the age of seven) who are being abused! Be the keeper of the secrets and live the true life of the spiritual person on a journey to the secret world."

I give thanks for my traditional and cultural training, my apprenticeship in Indian Medicine, and my experience in working with the United Methodist Mission in the Great Smoky Mountains. Each in its own way had secrets that sustained me during the Vietnam War and in choosing a career in Public Health with the Indian Health Service. It is with deep respect and appreciation to the Cherokee and other Native American Elders that I am thankful for their sharing and their support of me writing this book. While not mentioning their names, I honor their Medicine power. For those who have passed on to the other world, I honor their memories. As an Elder said, "There is a time for grief, and that must be done. We will all be on a different journey someday. There will be a time when you will be the one to share. Learn to honor the memories and let the rest go. A good way to honor that memory is to be a helper to others." You will now go with me through a journey of the Four Directions and experience each direction as we come together into the Universal Circle. We will be on the Good Medicine path of harmony and balance, and we will share the Native American purpose in being a keeper of the secrets and a protector of Mother Earth.

# Four Sacred Directions

This chapter focuses on the Native American teachings of the Four Directions. Then the chapters that follow describe each of the Four Directions, activities to honor them, and how the energy affects our lives.

The Four Cardinal Directions, as we call them, are what were called the "Cords of Life." Each cord or direction has its own energy. Some people have a pulling to one or the other, and some feel in between one and the other. Hopefully, they are somewhere in the circle. Of course, the directions have their opposite poles. That makes some people think they are going one way, when they are really going the other. Understanding these relationships is necessary in learning Indian Medicine, and these relationships are understood in lessons. Just like the lesson of the eagle feather, everything has two ways that are opposite. You should know that we are influenced by the directional energy and that not all opposites attract.

The Four Directions are the South, West, North, and

East. This clockwise circle represents the spiral of life with directional energy that influences our lives. The center of the Four Directions is the Universal Circle, which moves to infinity like rings of water when you toss a rock into a pool. Everything in the Cherokee Way or teachings begins with the fire in the center as the path to the Great One and the begin-

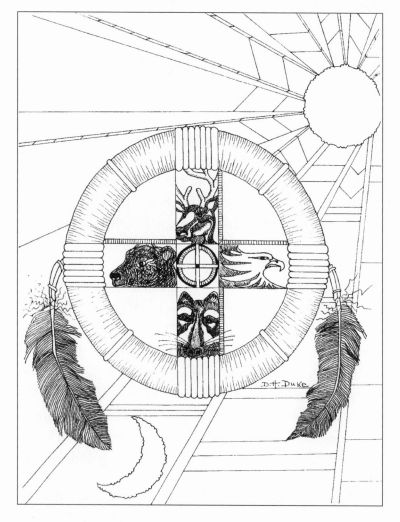

ning of all living things on Earth. Native Americans respect the council or circle gathering as a "coming together" to hear issues and for resolution, ceremony, and bonding of individual with family, clan, and tribe. The Council Fire is often symbolized in some way to remind us that the first council was around a fire. It also shows respect for the cultural traditions. The Four Directions represent the Cords of Life, or energies that influence and affect every part of our being.

As I was taught these lessons, I found myself having to shift to another level or place for understanding. I learned that the Cords of Life provide us with balance, while we maintain harmony with everything as the keepers of our Mother Earth. Our biggest concern right now is that we are affecting the balance of Earth by interfering with the energies and polluting the environment. While we cannot change the Four Directions, considerable concern was expressed by several Native Americans about the very serious effect of interfering with Earth's energy balance by introducing another energy such as nuclear radiation. The Elders also said that we feel the effects of every war for many generations, like a stone thrown into the water with rippling effects until Mother Earth is able to "clear" herself.

The Four Directions provide a helper to us for the understanding of our own behavior and direction. They provide a guide for us to find our place or spot in the energy balance. As the Elder said, "We need to get back to the Center Fire and get in touch with our spirit self, then find our place in the circle for peace of mind. The Directions provide us balance, but we have to find harmony in relationship to everything in our environment." The rest of this chapter is my journey through the experience of learning Indian Medicine.

It is necessary to remove our critical hats and just accept some ideas until we can decide what fits best in our lives. Many people tend to think of the environment as just air, water, and land mass. People tend to forget about the trees, plants, animals, birds, and synergistic harmony of all things. Maybe it is a good time to get back to the center of the circle and rekindle our sense of connection with Nature and our synergistic harmony with all things in the Universal Circle.

........................................................

## THE CENTER OF THE CIRCLE

The circle is considered by Native Americans as the Universal Circle with the Four Directions being identified on the Medicine Wheel. The Medicine Wheel represents the individual and the clan as lessons in life for directions and guidance for us to follow. This is as sacred as the other things that guide us. In Cherokee teachings, the number seven is considered sacred, or the Sacred Seven. With the Four Directions of South, West, North, and East as the sacred four, the number five is to be referred to as the Sun or the Upper World. The number six is considered to be Mother Earth, and the number seven as the sacred fire in the center of the circle. The Sacred Seven becomes our connection with the Great One in the Universal Circle. It becomes the center of us as the spirit self connected to the Universal Spirit.

Native American teachings say that we are all brothers and sisters to everything in the Universal Circle. When I was a young boy, my grandfather would say, "The plants are your brother and sisters, even the skunk is kin to you. We are all related and connected to each other." I was looking down at the rock by the river where we were sitting and said, "And even this rock?" "Especially this rock," said my grandfather. "Many of the things we learned, we learned from the rock. After all, Grandfather Rock was the first one here. His energy is so solid that we can stand on him. He is at peace when we lay in his lap. Here, try it." There was a rock with an indentation similar to a chair. As I lay there on the rock, I sensed a very peaceful feeling. My grandfather said, "When I was a boy and the chores would get too hard and I would be tired, I would do just as you are doing. You see, the rock has energy too, and that good energy makes you feel good. I used to know that I was protected by the rock. You can also talk to the rock." My eyes lit up. "Are you serious?" "Yep, but you have to know how to talk to the rock, just like you have to know how to talk to the animals in the woods.

"Pretend you are smiling, but don't show it on your face. Can you do that?" "Yea, I think so," I said as my eyes closed. With the water gurgling over the rocks and a slight breeze rustling the pines, I fell asleep. After a while I awoke and looked around to see my grandfather's big smile, and I smiled. "Oops, you were not to show me your smile." We laughed, and he said, "Well, you talked to the rock." "Yep, for a long time. I don't know what we talked about," I said with a curious thought in mind. "Well, I believe that is a secret between you and that old rock." "What did you do while I was talking to the rock?" I asked. My grandfather looked at me with a grin, "I was talking to the fish, 'cause I am fixin' to go get my fishing pole."

Native Americans honor these memories in giving thanks each day and in ceremonies for the lessons learned, and to be learned, from our Elders. The Four Directions give us direction in our lives, and these stories connect us, with a sense of being, to everything around us in the Universal Circle and to the power of the Great One.

In Native American teachings, the plants were here first; then came the birds and the animals. The human spirits were from spirits who were willing to share themselves so the humans could be physical and be the keepers of Mother Earth. We are considered as being much younger than the other spirits. That also means we have much yet to learn from the plants about taking care of our health; from the animals about survival; and from the birds about our spirit freedom.

Coming to the center of the circle connects us to the fire. The fire generates a spirit of action and inner-action with guidance. It raises our level of awareness and sensitivity to concerns that all of us have for harmony and balance in our lives. Coming to the center is also a way of saying that we must come together as people for action and resolution as helpers and protectors. We "center" ourselves to rebalance when we get "a little off kilter," as my father would say. It is also a way to emphasize that we get in touch with our deeper spirit self and to follow our gut feelings. Sharing about the teachings of energy and feelings gives us a better under-standing of the lessons from Native American ancestors that can help us be better helpers.

## THE RULE OF OPPOSITES

In Indian Medicine, energy is a continuum that does not change. We as energy beings have our own special vibra-tion, and we connect with other energy by a process of phas-ing our energy into our center or spirit self, then emerging or opening our hands to receive the energy of the Universal Circle. Instead of seeing energy as just being work, the elder teachers consider it associated with each of the Four Directions as physical, mental, spiritual, and natural. It can be directed, interfered with, and taught. This concept is not easy to teach others, except through exercises and what my son and I refer to as Full Circle gatherings. What I refer to as the Rule of Opposites has two lessons: first, to learn how to train oneself to use energy; and second, to understand that whatever we think or do, there is the opposite of that. To understand this lesson is to be aware that what we say or do may really mean the opposite of what we are meaning to say or do. The energy I am referring to will go through anything and is constantly around us as natural energy. Physical energy is caused by friction or electrical impulse, and the Elders refer to it as a lower level of energy. Mental energy is a form of communications or spirit energy that has memory. It is fairly easy to interfere with this energy, as it is a higher energy that goes "outside of the wires" (that is, extends outside the body the same way that electric energy can be detected outside electrical wires) due to a lower-frequency vibration in the body itself. The higher level of energy (spiritual and natural) is only possible to connect with when we spiral to a much higher level of calm and connection. Connecting with Mother Nature is the easiest way to reach this spiral and to become more sensitive to the feeling of energy differences.

The sacred items used with energy include such items as a power feather, a power stick, or a power crystal. Each of these items has the same four types of energy—physical, mental, spiritual, and natural—as does everything in Nature. Each of us also has a male and a female spirit energy. As an Elder said, "We are energy with connections with other energy. We are people polarized with opposite energy as well. Sometimes we think we are going in the right direction for us, when, in fact, we should be going in another direction. The white man's way is to control adversity; our way is to walk the peaceful path in harmony with our environment and to find the Good Medicine Way." This Elder was a female who told me a wonderful story about why the Sun rises in the East and sets in the West, and the relationship of the Sun and the Moon. The story goes as follows:

There was a time when the Sun was very young, and she lived in the East. There was a young man who would come to visit with her in the evening, maybe this was the beginning of courting. She thought it was strange that he would always leave near daylight. They would talk and stare at the beautiful stars in the deep universal skyvault. While she could talk with him, she could not see him. He would not even tell her his name. Out of curiosity, she decided to find out who he really was by touching him in the dark of night. As on every night in the past, he came to see her saying very nice things to her about how bright her smile was and how she was so round and perfect. While sitting in the dark, she reached her hand into some warm ashes from an earlier fire. She said, "You are very cold from the wind hitting your face. Here, let me warm your face," as she put the ashes on his face. He did not know that she had ashes on her hands, as she was pretending to feel sorry for him. At the first peek of daylight, he abruptly left on his journey.

When the Moon came up in the skyvault the next day, the young Sun could see the ashes on his face. Then she could see that it was her brother, the Moon, who was coming to see her. While she was excited to see who he was, she also knew that the Moon was her brother. The Moon felt ashamed, and to this day comes up at the other end of the skyvault to keep his distance from the Sun going down.

While the story is used to teach values, it is also told to help us better understand energies. Not all opposites attract, though certainly some attract, but show their face later. While we are all brothers and sisters, there is an attraction that is Good Medicine. While things are not always as simple as "attract and repel," the Rule of Opposites helps us to understand the point of differences in energy.

A friend of mine worked very hard to be the best sales-man, to make a lot of money for his family, and to have what he called "the good life." Both of us were from tribes on res-ervations. I sensed that he was going in one direction but really wanted to be in another, and I talked to an Elder about this situation. My fear was that I might be doing the same thing he was doing. The Elder said, "Sometimes the Amer-ican dream is also the American nightmare. The Indian way is to help our brothers and sisters and to care for those who cannot care for themselves. It is about giving, but it does not mean that we cannot have 'the good life.' It is a matter of what is meant by 'good life' versus Good Medicine Way. You must follow your vision." The friend died at an early age of a massive heart attack, and I felt guilty because I did not try to change his mind. The Elder said, "You cannot change some-one's energy, only interfere with it, and you could take on their consequences. You must be careful about these things and remember your teachings! The direction he was really seeking was the calm of the mountains, while he perused the city—it was his choice."

Our feelings, like the young Sun and Moon, tend to draw us toward someone or something. The Rule of Opposites teaches us that energy can reverse itself, as it has done with Mother Earth many times over the past four billion years or more. Influences can be very strong, but we still must follow our gut feelings and spirit guidance to be sure that the path is Good Medicine. As an Elder said, "Is it the vision of reality or nonreality that we seek to find? Use the *feel* of energy to see if it really attracts or actually repels once the energy is mixed. Remember the lesson of the mask as you meet people who present themselves as someone other than who they really are. Seek a vision that is real and of truth, not of consequences." He also spoke of two persons very much in love, who could hate each other very much, given consequences and circumstances. The point was that the "feel" of energy is something to be learned in life, while understanding the Rule of Opposites.

The Rule of Opposites can be used as an "energy-check" to see if the direction we are going is really where we want to be. Sometimes we can be going in entirely the wrong direction and projecting our reason as an excuse to drink or whatever. These are the "I have to do this because . . ." people or the "I don't have any choice" people or the "He (or she) made me do it" people. A good energy-check is to ask an Elder or your family about the choices you make. Another is to just sit within the energies of Nature, under a tree or in a setting with plants. Breathe in and out several times and focus on turning inward toward the heart or the gut, and just ask where you should go or what you should do. Once you have gone through the Four Directions, you will better understand the Rule of Acceptance and the Rule of Opposites.

••••••••••••••••••••••••••••••••••••••••••••••••••••••••

### LESSON FROM OUR ANCESTORS

One of the Cherokee Elders often spoke about the emergence of teachings coming from the Four Directions. He said that some Medicine Men refer to the period today as a cycle that started in 1994, as the emergence of a new Sun gave us new direction and the integration of a renewed understanding. A renewed healing will begin taking place that will overshadow the misunderstandings of the past four centuries. Some of the Native Americans and traditional healers have been willing to meet in joint sessions with the United Nations and other national and international organizations to call attention to concerns about our environment and survival of life on our Mother Earth. Unlike the messages of gloom and doom, their messages are generally about the need for renewal, clearing, and revival of the traditional cultural ways to be helpers in this renewed healing.

It is wonderful to see the "coming out" and sharing of the traditional knowledge, stories, and wisdom by Native Americans today. The Elder, in speaking to me about these concerns said, "We must share the truth, because there is so much untruth based on greed and possession of something. My time has come and gone; now it is time for you and others to become the Elders with a message, a prayer, and a vision. Tell them (all people) that we (Native Americans) have been on this Earth Mother for a long time. We know her signs, and she is hurting. They must help her, and pray for her, and you must be a keeper and sharer of the wisdom."

..........................................................

## CHOOSING A DIRECTION

A young boy was sitting in the middle of a path that crossed in the directions of North and South, East and West. The Medicine Elder said to the boy, "Why are you sitting in the path?" The boy said, "I don't know which direction is the right one for me to follow. I have been sitting here for many passing of the moons, and it has not come to me. Are you willing to help me?" The Elder told the boy the stories taught to him by the Grandfathers and Grandmothers about life and the Four Directions, about the Universal Circle and giving thanks to the Great One. The young boy realized that it was not his time to go away from his village. He realized that, in giving thanks each day to the rising Sun, he would be guided when the time was right for his journey into life. The Elder shared a "Clearing Way" chant and how to perform a "Blessing Way" chant to share with other young people, to guide them and to teach them the values of life. The young boy learned respect for all his brothers and sisters, particularly the Elders, and then the Elder was gone.

As the boy shared what had happened and told of the Medicine Elder, the people were surprised. They had not heard of this Elder, and he had not come through the village in his travels. The young boy was told that he had had a vision and that a "spirit teacher" had come to him. My teachers said that choosing the directions at the right time would come in "small pieces," or like a film rolling in front of us when we would least expect it. The activity would be to meditate in the calming energy of a tree or a garden of plants and flowers to "quiet the mind and to listen to the heart."

The journey through the Four Directions will be to find your own place where there is a sense of harmony and balance. As you read the chapters on each of the Four Directions, consider which direction "feels" most comfortable to you. You may feel a little between two of them, but still choose one that seems to fit you at that moment the best. We will start the journey in the direction of the South.

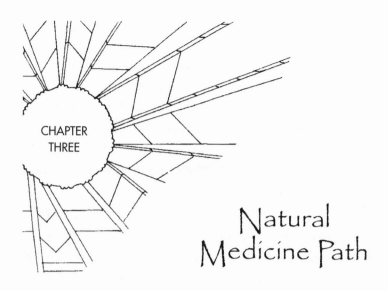

# Natural Medicine Path

The direction of the South is the Nature path where the spirit being becomes a human being. The color of the South is usually white to represent purity, or green to represent plants. "The spirit one comes to the earth plane through the sacred center and passes through the Thunder Beings in the East for Good Medicine power, then is born into Nature as pure as the innocence of the South." That means the little ones are to be treated as sacred little persons to be nurtured and protected until they reach the age of seven. "Until then, they have a close connection to the spirit world and will even remember things of the other world," says the Medicine Elder.

People that seem to best fit in the direction of the South seek to retain or regain their innocence. They like to play games, and they focus on peaceful thoughts and caring for animals and others. The friendship circle is always found here, and becomes a way of coming together, sharing, dancing, and singing.

Children and adults enjoy the drumming and the slow dancing of the circle; they hold hands and go around and around until they come together into the center, and this is called the Friendship Dance. They also enjoy the Snake Dance with faster drumming where a lead dancer pulls the circle in different directions. The sense of inner-connection is important, as is the sense of fair play. The circle, council, or gathering—sometimes referred to as a "coming together"— provides a sense of support, and folks here tend to stick together. Traditional Native American dances used a slow heel-toe step or involved just sliding the feet within the circle. Children would dance the Beaver Dance and imitate hunting the rabbit and deer. *Interdependence* within families, clans, and tribes, as well as *activity* and *expression,* were encouraged in the direction of the South.

While teaching me about the direction of the South, an Elder said, "The South is warm, slow-paced, like the hearts of its people. In the old days, the South could be harsh with lots of bugs and critters that would eat you alive, or at least 'bug' you to death. My grandma would put bear grease on us to drive away the bugs. 'Course, it drove away everybody else too. That's the reason I didn't have a girlfriend until I moved back to the mountains, where we didn't have bugs flying around like they did in Florida. Anyway, the beginning of disease and medicine started in this direction." This chapter will emphasize the natural aspects of our lives, like when we were children and enjoyed playing outside in Nature.

In a different time, everything lived in the circle of friendship, and everyone got along just fine. As the story goes, there was no war, conflict, or violence. From the story of the beginning, the human beings used their abilities for

protection to make sharp objects of flint and wood. With
these arrows and spears, they would stalk and kill the animals
and fish. It was alright for the human being to take the life of
an animal being, but he or she had to ask the animal spirit for

permission and to give thanks. Permission was given as long as the hunter and his family were hungry and needed the skin for warmth. However, the human beings began to kill without permission and even when their bellies were full. It was time for the animals to call a council. The bears and the deer knew that they would share themselves, but they wanted the humans to ask if it was alright to take the lives of the animals and to give thanks to the Great One. The animals wanted the humans only to take what was needed for their families to live. If this was not done, then the deer spirit would cause the humans to have rheumatism. While the deer was good meat to eat, it was also one of the sacred animals. The bear spirit would cause the hunter to have a crippled walk and arthritis to stop the humans from killing so many of the animals.

As the story goes, the snakes made the humans dream of things to lose their appetite. The humans stepped on the backs of the frogs until they (the frogs) had sores on their backs. The birds said that their feet would be burned by the fire, and their remains were left all over the ground, instead of being treated with respect. There were several councils until many diseases were devised to teach the humans to respect their brothers and sisters put here on Mother Earth. The plants met in council because they felt sorry for the humans who would not pray and show respect to all of Nature. From that time on, every plant and even the moss found a way to help teach humans how to heal from the illnesses and diseases. The Great One looking down thanked the plants and forgave all of the animals for their council action. He decided that the humans should learn respect for all things on Mother Earth, but asked the plants to be helpers whenever the humans would ask. The male human is sometimes stubborn, so the spirits of the plants decided to help him treat his illness, but only when he asked and gave thanks in prayer chants. The female human was chosen as the teacher to pass the Medicine along to generation after generation to prevent disease and illness by using the plant helpers. And, as the Elder said, "This was told by the Ancient Ones. If you don't believe me, try not eating plants and see what happens."

...................................................

## LEARNING TO BE HELPERS

The plants decided to be helpers to humans who were getting sick from their own misguided actions. Helpers can also be humans helping other humans to aid the healing in a variety of ways. As an Elder said, "The Great One gave us a 'sense of knowing' from our spirit memory that we don't use very much these days. It's like we know that we know, but we are too lazy sometimes to seek it out. The animals, well, they just do what they need to do. As humans, we want someone else to do it for us, but we do have the Medicine power in each of us." She went on to tell the story of the origin of Medicine.

The plants had a special relationship with Mother Earth, as the story goes, to give life and oxygen for the animals and humans to breathe. In the presence of the Sun, they developed many varieties with different energies and shapes so that humans could recognize them. The humans did very well at deciding names based on the shapes. The Plant Clan in council decided that it would be helpful to have different tastes and colors because the humans were still young and had a lot to learn. One plant said, "I will be a bright purple and make myself like a horn so they can see me in the dark." We call them nightshades. Of course, this was a very long council, as the plants decided ways to have presence for the humans to learn the Medicine. After all, the Great One intended for the humans to be the keepers of Mother Earth. It was decided in the council of the Plant Clan for all plants to be helpers to the human spirits from that day forward.

"Most people do not remember this, but there was a test of endurance and vision," said the Elder. "The plants and animals were given a chance to test their endurance in staying awake while praying to the Great One during the long evenings. All the animals fell asleep, with the exception of the owl and the panther. So, they were given the power to see in the dark and to continue their prayers so others could sleep at night. Of the plants, only the nightshade plants and the trees of cedar, pine, holly, and laurel were still awake. So, they were given the special color to always be green and have powerful Medicine."

Our connection with all of life is stored in the memories in each cell and in the messages within each molecule. The researchers call it DNA, and it controls replication of itself through genes. We are of organic and inorganic compounds like our brothers and sisters in Nature. It has been estimated that there are over 350,000 species of plants and some 6000 species of ferns. The Rule of Opposites also applies to the relationship that plants and trees have with humans and animals. We breathe in oxygen and breathe out carbon dioxide. The plant takes in carbon dioxide and gives off oxygen. Can you imagine what we are doing by cutting down all of our trees and destroying our rain forests? Our entire environ-mental integrity and life itself are threatened, as are the plants, animals, birds, and Mother Earth herself. While ani-mals ingest food and break it down into molecules, plants build food from molecules in the presence of sunlight. We need each other for survival of Mother Earth.

..........................................................

### GETTING BACK TO OUR "ROOTS"

Our survival may well depend on natural herbs and plants as the cures for AIDS and other killers yet to come. It has been said that 10 percent or less of the more than 350,000 plant species are known by us. Our concerns for such killers as AIDS started us looking again at natural plants, rather than only at synthetics. Automated methods today allow us to test thousands of samples each year. The botanical and pharma-ceutical companies' research labs have initiated many plant-screening programs for treatment and research drugs for clinical trials. The National Cancer Institute has reviewed approximately 23,000 samples from close to 7000 species in tropical areas for compounds to treat AIDS and to find treat-ments for cancer and other diseases.

I appreciate the modern pharmacy and homeopathy treatments. At the same time, none of us as Native Americans wants to give up our natural remedies and the tra-ditional gifts of nature given to us from the Elders. Can you imagine what would happen to our beautiful dogwood trees if we had no aspirin today, and people knew that the dog-wood bark contained salicin that is the main agent in aspirin? We would not have any dogwood left. Our natural pharmacy must be protected from poachers and abusers of Mother

Earth. As the first naturalists, environmentalists, and conservationists here in America, Native Americans accept the role of keepers and protectors of Earth Mother. Of course, many of us recognize that people from every culture, including some Native Americans, abuse or allow abuse of our natural resources.

It is important for every child to learn the natural lessons of life such as planting trees and flowers, growing corn and other foods, and sharing with others when we have too much. Planting trees and caring for plants and flowers can build self-esteem and bonding with family and clans or extended families and communities. They also should learn self-care and survival, other than on the city streets. It is really a good feeling to see a small child plant a seed, grow the plant, and then be able to eat the fruit off the vine. The same is true with simply cutting the eye of a potato and planting it in some soft ground, then watching the child dig up a whole potato! Even from survival on the streets, children can learn to be helpers too.

We as humans have been around for many generations of learning and sharing. It has been estimated that Earth is some 4.6 billion years old. The earliest signs of life on Earth are in rocks about 3.5 to 3.8 billion years old. As humans, we have managed to destroy natural resources at astounding rates. The "Greenhouse Effect" is a way to keep plants warm in a constructed greenhouse. In Nature, the gases going toward the sky form a clear blanket that allows sunlight to enter and reach Earth's surface, but prevents the heat buildup from escaping. This warms the atmosphere and keeps heat close to the surface. We are altering the climate by increasing the total amount of carbon dioxide in the atmosphere, which is estimated to be about 25 percent more today than it was less than two centuries ago. These gases come from burning fossil fuels and trees—the same trees so desperately needed for producing oxygen. This is a critical time for us to be helpers in a personal, get-involved way, rather than staying out of the way. As a Cherokee Elder said, "The answer is simple. Stop the waste and return to the natural ways of harmony and balance, post haste!"

Getting back to our "roots" means getting back to the simple lifestyle of conserving energy and reducing waste. It also means getting back to our natural gift of planting and growing, rather than just opening cans for food to eat. It means starting to learn some simple herbal and natural remedies and treatments, particularly for young children, so they can pass these wonderful gifts along to the future generations .

Our "roots" will always go back to the plants given to feed us and to be helpers for curing ills and protecting our well-being. It has been estimated that about one fourth of our current prescription drugs in the United States contain at least one compound derived from plants. There is no telling how many ideas for drug therapies have also been derived from microbes and variants from the massive data banks of information. As predicted by Native Americans, the white man's appetite for more and more, particularly with drugs, has led to a whole industry of manufacturing synthetic drugs. It was also understood that these "bullets," as one Elder calls them, would not be the total answer, because they do not consider the total person and this person's environment. It is time for an emerging Medicine way with a natural flow to bring about a renewed sense of harmony and balance. It is time for us to remember again what we already know in spirit memory.

· · · · · · · · · · · · · · · · · · · · · · · · · · · · · · · · · · · · · · · · · · · · · · · · · · · · · · · ·

### HERBAL AND NATURAL GIFTS

In the Cherokee traditions, corn was a integral part of the stories or myths as well as a staple food. While there are many stories how the corn came to be, the myth is that the first woman or Corn Maiden grew out of this stalk of corn from the dream and heart of a man who made the commitment to the Great One to provide for and shelter a maiden to love. At the top of the stalk of corn was a beautiful woman that the man realized was not a dream at all. They went to make a home and plant a garden. The first woman wanted to take some of the corn with her as a reminder of her heritage. She kept four ears from the stalk, which was called "se-lu" or the first corn. At first, she did not know that the corn was to eat, so she planted it like flowers, which grew beautiful yellow-gold corn that would glisten in the sunlight.

The first woman looked at a beautiful corn "flower" one early morning to find a bird eating the seeds of the corn. She thought, if the bird called a wild turkey could eat it, then so could humans. Since then, corn has been roasted, popped like popcorn, made into cornbread, and ground into corn meal, and even used in ceremonies with the sacred fire to honor this Cherokee tradition. Of course, the Cherokee also like to boil it with hardwood ashes to make hominy and to grind it into grits. Se-lu has been a part of the food and Medicine since the beginning of the Corn Maiden.

••••••••••••••••••••••••••••••••••••••••••••••••••

## A FEW GOOD HERBS

We spend some $1 trillion on disease treatment in the United States. These costs for health care consume more of our Gross National Product than ever before. The cost of prescription drugs, like the cost of many vitamins, has also skyrocketed in recent years. This does not mean that many of these high-cost vitamins are any better than the simple plant remedies put together by our grandfathers and grandmothers. While supplements are very necessary for some people, I really encourage fresh vegetables whenever possible for the antioxidant vitamins that include vitamins C, E, and A (beta-carotene). Vitamin C is in fruits and vegetables such as grapefruit, oranges, strawberries, and potatoes. Vitamin E is in nuts, certain vegetable oils, and leafy greens. Beta-carotene is in dark-green leafy vegetables such as collard greens and spinach, and can be found in cantaloupes, peaches, carrots, and sweet potatoes. These antioxidant vitamins are for protection of the cells and to neutralize free radicals, which are very reactive and unstable molecules that cause cell damage. It is possible for the cellular damage and other toxic influences to cause or predispose us to chronic diseases such as cancer and heart disease. The antioxidant vitamins can be helpers to prevent the damage caused by free radicals and to help prevent some chronic diseases.

The natural Medicine of the South is related to herbs and plant foods that are helpers for us to grow, stay healthy, and be protected, just as a parent watches over a child. These natural herbs and remedies are, as our grandmother says, "what's good for us." I will list a few of these good herbs that are special to me and always available in my

Medicine Bag. Begin or expand your Medicine Bag with a few herbs that focus on some recurring condition or experience. Next, try some of these herbs or natural foods until you are comfortable with them. Of course, make sure that the use of these herbs does not interfere with any medications you are currently taking. Ask someone at the health-food store or the pharmacy about taking an herb with certain medications in order to avoid interference with the potency and effect of the medication you are taking. As one Elder put it, "Powerful plant spirits are helpers to the human spirits." Therefore, we must learn about the special relationship of these helpers to one another and to us. Some herbs enhance and others interfere. Some herbs calm, while others stimulate.

I would encourage you to find your own seven or twelve sacred and food-related herbs for Good Medicine. The number "seven" is considered sacred among the Cherokee. Therefore, seven herbs or foods such as onions or carrots could be a regular part of the Medicine each day for good health. I use "twelve" as a way to balance the body and spirit as a complete cycle or circle for harmony and balance. This is similar to the Cherokee idea of a complete circle of healing.

••••••••••••••••••••••••••••••••••••••••••••••••••••••••

## MEDICINE OF THE SOUTH

The natural Medicine of the South is associated with stimulating the system for play and competition, clearing and absorption, protective remedies, and rest and recovery. Some of the most powerful herbs are in the direction of the Natural or the South.

This direction represents the beginning of life, with

powerful energy connected with the spirit because of the closeness of the body and spirit in this direction.

**Aloe (Aloe vera)**—While traded in earlier years and not native to America, aloe made its way into the Indian Medicine remedies. It is easy to grow and just continues to proliferate. The fresh juice makes an excellent salve for burns. The mucilaginous gel in the center of the leaf is aloe gel. My grandfather used it with another substance for warts, but sometimes he would just use the aloe on a cotton swab, changing it every few hours over a period of four days, then keeping a gel cotton on until the wart would disappear without any trace of scar tissue. It is my understanding that aloe vera contains about 96 percent water and the remainder is the natural substance called aloin. The gel penetrates the human skin almost four times faster than water, making it an excellent moisturizer for our skin. While we did not use it orally, I do understand that studies have been done to show that aloe can enhance the immune system as an extract called manapol that somehow stimulates the production of macrophages, interferon, and lymphocytes, while having other positive effects. The potential for healing using this substance for ulcerative colitis and other internal damage has excellent promise as it is both an antiviral and antifungal substance. This is a healing herb that my mother always kept in our home.

**Balm (Melissa officinalis)**—This plant has been used as a calming sedative for many generations in my family. Also called **lemon balm**, it is good as a "sipping tea" with some honey to sooth the throat and to calm the system. Place some chopped leaves into a cup of boiling water as a balm tea, or just add the leaves to your favorite tea for a mild and calm taste. When we named our daughter Melissa, I thought of her as my little flower girl. She has always loved plants and knowing how to use them, and lemon is one of her favorite flavors for just about everything. Like the plant, she was a special gift and helper.

**Burdock (Arctium lappa)**—This is one of the best "washes" for treating sores and abrasions of the skin and for poison ivy. In earlier years when folks used their hands a lot in farming, they would not be without it. Well, it feels good even today to mix some comfrey and burdock as a mild wash for the hands, then rub a mild moisturing cream on them, just to pamper yourself. The Cherokee used burdock as a tea to eliminate poisons in the stomach and to stimulate the secretion of bile for cleaning the liver. A mild tea is good for an upset stomach. Prepare the tea by placing a teaspoon of the ground root in a cup of cold water and let it stand overnight before drinking. Add two cups of distilled water and bring to a boil. Cool it down and you then have a "wash."

**Comfrey or Healing Herb (Symphytum officinale)**— Truly a healing herb, comfrey is used in many ways from wounds of the skin to internal problems. The Cherokee used it with boneset as a healing agent for broken bones. I use it externally only, as it contains allantoin, which is good for skin rashes. Comfrey mixed with the juice of a broadleaf plantain leaf makes a good skin ointment for enhancing the healing process of wounds on skin; the plantain is a good natural antiseptic. Comfrey is always in my Medicine Bag. I do cau-

tion you to be sure that in the wild you don't choose fox-
glove, thinking it is comfrey, since they are similiar-looking
plants.

**Cucumber (Cucumis satirus)**—In earlier years, cucumber was used by the Cherokee and others practicing folk
medicine for heart and kidney problems and edema or
swelling, and for dissolving uric acid accumulations related
to kidney and bladder stones. I have used it as a natural
diuretic by eating the entire cucumber. Cucumbers make a
wonderful and refreshing snack while helping the system get
rid of toxins and poisons that have accumulated, particularly
during and after having colds and the flu. Try placing a slice
on a sore or a burn with aloe vera, or placing a slice on your
tired eyes for a cooling and refreshed feeling. Be sure to use
a cucumber that is fully ripe and starting to turn yellow.

**Dandelion (Taraxacum officinale)**—A favorite for
many Cherokee, it is still used in salads to add taste and as a
good "blood tonic." It is also a good natural diuretic with
plenty of nutrients. The early Cherokee considered it as an
Indian "one-a-day" natural plant. The leaves are usually col-
lected before flowering as salad greens. It is rich in vitamins
A and C. While I have not tasted dandelion wine, I have used
the dried roots roasted with chicory added to make a natural
coffee. The leaves were used in earlier years for ailments of
the liver and gallbladder, and other digestive problems.

**Garlic (Allium satirum)**—While it has many uses, I use
it as an internal antiseptic cleanser and for colds. I also use it
as a helper for lowering my cholesterol, reducing blood pres-

sure, and protecting against bacterial and fungal infections. While it contains allicin as the substance that gives it the classic odor, some researchers say that oxidization occurs with its use, which makes it a good substance with many active ingredients. As my grandmother used to say, "Eat a piece of garlic and you won't get a cold. In fact, no one will get even close enough to you to give you a cold!"

**Ginger or Wild Ginger (Asarum canadense)**—This herb was used for settling the stomach and as a diuretic for colds by Native Americans. Today it is used in foods and to stimulate digestion. As an Elder said, "Ginger is a special little plant with bright green leaves that wave to you as you walk in the damp and shaded areas in the mountains. It is there to teach us, to stimulate our learning and appetite." To prepare ginger tea, mix a half-teaspoon of the powdered rootstock with a teaspoon of honey in a cup of hot water and sip slowly.

**Mints (Memtha piperita or M. spicata)**—Both peppermint and spearmint are carminatives to calm the stomach and digestive system as very good herbal teas. I keep some of both in my Medicine Bag for aroma, along with sage and sweetgrass. This is a good herb to teach children to recognize and to appreciate because of the particular aroma and its safe use with food and teas. Collect some mint leaves on a warm day before the plant begins to flower. Cut the leaves so you have two teaspoons per cup of cold or hot water as a drink. I like to just cut a leaf and put it in my regular tea to steep for flavor.

**Onion (Allium cepa)**—This layered ground bulb is used primarily in cooked foods, but it is also a very good helper. It is especially useful for improving digestion and to calm the stomach or the intestines. It is used for helping lower blood pressure. If you get a sore throat, try mixing the juice of a crushed onion with lemon and honey, and taking a spoonful or less. The Cherokee pick wild onion or "ramp" as a "spring tonic and cleanser" and as a food. It is rich in vitamins B and C, as well as considered an excellent antiseptic for external use on the skin. Eat the onion raw or place a teaspoon of chopped onion in a cup of water, soak overnight, and use as a Good Medicine drink.

**Plantain (Plantago major)**—The common plantain is a familiar broadleaf plant that grows just about anywhere in lawns, fields, and roadsides. An Elder referred to it as an "Indian bandaid," probably due to the natural antiseptic quality of a crushed fresh leaf placed on a cut. The Cherokee would chew on a small piece of the fresh rootstock of this special healing plant for curing a toothache. They would also make a tea of the leaves for bladder problems and for bouts of gastrointestinal ulcers. The tea was prepared with a teaspoon of fresh or dried leaves in a cup of boiling water. While there are many good antiseptic products on the market, I like to share this little helper with children to give them a sense of survival confidence. They really enjoy learning how to use Mother Nature's gifts.

**Yellow Root or Goldenseal (Hydrastic canadensis)**—This was a plant commonly found on the creek banks in the Southeast and is an herb that I use for sore throats, which are recurrent for me due to public speaking and presentations. Often identified as a yellow-colored root used for making dye, goldenseal was used for ulcers in the mouth as a natural antiseptic and for stopping external bleeding. An alkaloid is extracted from the root for use in some types of eye drops. When I brew goldenseal as a tea, I take it for stomachaches in small quantities using the rhizome or rootstock. I do caution about taking goldenseal in large quantities because it can be poisonous. Seek advice from an herbalist or a naturopath regarding its use.

[Author's Note: *There are cautions in selecting your own herbs, and I would advise everyone to confer with someone who knows herbs and the possible complications with current drug therapies.* Comfrey tea has been implicated in liver disease due to alkaloids, and it was banned in Canada. Another example, the oil of sassafras, called "safrole,"was taken out of root beer about 30 years ago, but many Native Americans really like their sassafras drink.]

Early Cherokee on their travels to the ocean would collect two other Natural Medicine herbs: **kelp** (various types of seaweed) and **shells**, which were used as decorations hung around the neck and also ground up as a powder for taking internally. Of course, we know this today as calcium. The chlorophyll plants like kelp heal the mucous linings of the intestines, and were used for skin ulcers and detoxification of organs, particularly the liver. Physicians and dentists have used chlorophyll for treating oral diseases, kidney stones, and acute infections of the upper respiratory tract and sinuses. We now know that kelp, due to its iodine content, improves thyroid function and contains vitamins and minerals such as calcium, magnesium, potassium, niacin, riboflavin, and choline.

I should also mention that in Cherokee Medicine several herbs are usually used together based on natural balance and harmony for healing in the body. This is a sacred area that is very protected by clans and families. Our health is sacred to us. A certain Medicine may be handed down and provided by a tribal member or by many tribal members, instead of only being learned by the Medicine Man or Woman. The focus is on prevention and protection, rather than on the concept of treatment or disease control.

........................................................

### THE EMERGING MEDICINE WAY

The term "Medicine" is considered as power, as a path, and sometimes as magic, but always with choice(s) made by the individual, family, clan, and tribe, according to Indian Medicine teachings. Individual power is not something to be given away or interfered with, and each person has his or her own Medicine Bundle or special things considered sacred. I have a power feather, a power crystal, a power spot or place, a power song, and other things that are sacred to me as a Cherokee. These special items are a part of my Medicine Bag or Bundle. I accept the Western or allopathic medicine "disease theory" based on some external cause or agent that makes a person ill. However, my traditional teachings provide me with an appreciation of external things or experiences that interfere with my life energy. My life energy is physical, mental, spiritual, and natural. I look to my "Medicine" alongside of modern medicine—and sometimes *without* the modern medicine—to protect me and to be a helper for healing. How these agents or disease conditions are affecting me depends on what I do to gain Energy Medicine or to balance my male and female energies. The seeking and finding of whatever it takes to bring about this harmony puts me back on the path of Good Medicine.

The general concepts and ideas practiced and lived in Indian Medicine seem to be emerging in the ideas of today's "Energy Medicine." Indian Medicine does not forsake all the modern allopathic treatment modalities or ways, but allows for other "ways" that are sometimes referred to as "alternative and complementary." Indian Medicine is a gift and a choice of life. The emergence of Energy Medicine, now and in the future, takes into consideration many forms of treatment or choices that restore harmony and balance. Among the "alternative medicines" reviewed by the Office of Alternative Medicine at the National Institutes of Health are nutrition, health education, lifestyle modifications, biofeedback, relaxation techniques, acupuncture, homeopathy, herbal medicine, acupressure, spinal manipulation, massage, anti-oxidant therapy, bioelectromagnetic therapies, and other healing approaches or modalities. In addition, there are other therapies that will be included in the Energy Medicine model that includes herbal, hydrotherapy, hypnotherapy, metabolic therapy, naturopathic, yoga, reflexology, psychotherapy, podiatry, osteopathic medicine, orthomolecular therapy, psychic healing, spiritual healing, optometry, midwifery, and dentistry as a truly whole body-mind-spirit approach, given the total environment and all influences. The changing medical and health paradigm offers a future that we can all admire in bringing choice back to our own personal Medicine power.

......................................................

## SAVE AND SURVIVE

The Direction of the Natural is Mother Earth herself and our environment. This gives us a chance to be nature's helper. There are approximately three million to thirty million total plants, animals, and other species in the world. While numbers often conflict, it is estimated that there are some ten million species of land-dwelling animals. The basis of the food chain, photosynthetic plants provide the raw organic materials that form the first link in the food chain. These plants have to deal with almost ten times their number of insect species. The survival of food plants has recently been made dependent on insecticides and pesticides; both have harmful effects in the groundwater supply while controlling the destruction of our plants. Some environmentalists fear that eradication programs of earlier years may have also resulted in new strains and species surviving the original species of insects. We have managed to provide a progressive and hi-tech resolution to the massive feeding of our population, while causing an imbalance and a disharmony to our ecosystem. As we have found over and over again, the instinct to survive, whether it be that of an insect or a youth in an inner-city environment of crime and unemployment, takes precedence over all reason and is without respect for others. As the Elders teach us, the key is in finding a balance and harmony that is natural, to whatever extent possible.

For our benefit, we do have the National Environmental Policy Act that was signed into law in 1970 requiring environmental impact statements to protect the "quality of the human environment." It also preserves important natural aspects of our natural heritage. The Endangered Species Act of 1973 provides conservation legislation for the protection of plants and animals that are placed on the official roster of endangered species. The listing began in 1977, which meant that a beautiful little plant with maplelike leaves and clusters of greenish-white tubular flowers could be protected. It is called the miccosukee or Florida gooseberry (*Ribes echinellum*), a tiny shrub that is protected by the U.S. Fish and Wildlife Service. Somehow it survived as a species similar to one found almost 200 miles away in South Carolina. My main interest is in looking at the dramatic devastation of the beautiful pines and other trees in the Great Smoky Mountains and along the chain of Appalachian Mountains due to acid rain that is 10 times more acidic than in lower elevations and 100 times more than unpolluted rain. According to the World Resources Institute, acid rain at some mountain locations in the eastern United States has been measured as 2000 times more acidic than unpolluted rainwater. When compared to clear and clean rainwater, acid rain is like pouring lemon juice on the vegetation.

What can we do? As human beings of choice, we can do plenty! We can teach our children, and ourselves as adults, to go back to our roots: to plant and protect our trees and herbs; to recycle; to learn how to compost our organic garbage; to understand the environmental issues; and to protect the rain forests for our climate and our "breath of life," and to have all of us make a difference as keepers of Mother Earth. As an Elder put it, "If our plants and trees are diseased, then so are we, 'cause we share the energy that the Great One has put on Mother Earth. The Medicine Wheel is a spiral of transformation for us all. One does not exist without the other. We are all in this together." Probably, the best thing we can do is to get more involved as an individual, a family, and community in a local, national, and global way to share information, education, and understanding for solutions and resolutions. In the Native American Way, we can "come together" into councils like small local "clans" to share our energies toward choosing a path of Good Medicine, which results in action and interaction toward universal harmony and balance.

........................................................

## THE NATURAL MEDICINE

The interdependence of the physical, mental, spiritual, and natural aspects leads us to a way of better understanding how to pursue natural Medicine for our health and healing. It is about choice. Our health paradigm is changing from cause-and-effect and "do no harm" to harmony and balance and "do some good." The line in the television series, *Kung-Fu*, in which David Carradine says, "My name is Caine, I will help you," is the right approach. This is the Native American traditional approach as taught in the stories, that we are "helpers." The Cherokee were among many tribes that contributed remedies and herbs to the "Green Pharmacy."

Appalachian folk medicine brought us many remedies for "curing the ills of folks," as my grandmother used to say. Garlic to fight colds; tea bags for canker sores; baking soda for itches; and ginger for digestion and for calming the stomach—these are a few of the many remedies used by my mother, aunt, grandmother, and many others in the mountains of the southeastern United States. Ice was the "cure-all" when I was growing up because it was used to relieve insect bites, sinuses, toothaches, pain, and swelling. Simple remedies such as these, and the ones I described earlier, have a reasonable basis as long as they do no harm and do promote the healing process. Like Caine in *Kung-Fu*, the helpers in the physical, mental, spiritual, and natural aspects are available for the seeking and the vision.

There are some natural herbs that can be found in Nature's medicine cabinet of Mother Earth. Many people ask, "What herbs should I use or where should I go for help?" In the Native American Way, each person learns about certain natural and herbal remedies from their family and clans. The next sources would be their own teachers; Medicine persons; grandfathers and grandmothers as "special" persons or beloved Elders; and, finally, educational materials. I have my own cadre of herbs and natural ways that have been shared, and my own experience. I would also caution you to seek carefully to avoid the "land mines" of toxic substances—either in or on the plants, due to pollution—and to use fresh organic vegetables whenever possible. Start growing your own, and you will share energy in the process!

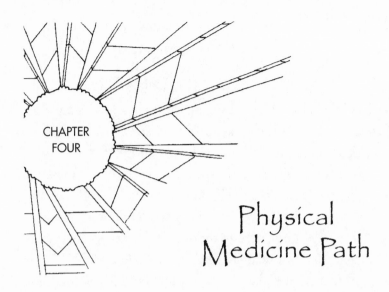

# Physical
# Medicine Path

The Physical is the direction of the West. Early Native American teachings would relate to the West as the direction of the "darkened land." Black is usually the color associated with the sacred and the West. The West is sometimes referred to with such animal names as bear, buffalo, or wolf. To Native Americans, the West is often related to endurance, physical beauty, competition, and introspection. The West was associated with the physical path and with spiraling to reach adulthood in the North.

The West can be thought of as a direction of adolescence in life and learning how to best utilize our physical gifts. An Elder said, "The direction of the West is sorta' like us focusing on our physical bodies or self that makes us worry about how we look and feel. It is also the endurance of life to reach adulthood and maturity. There is also a delicate balance between the physical life and the afterlife that we must learn to better appreciate the lessons learned and what we must do in this life to help others."

For the direction of the West, the Rule of Opposites would indicate that the direction of the East or spiritual activities would help to balance the physical aspect. A young man came to see one of my teachers about some bad dreams of snakes trying to get him and people beating him up. He was losing sleep and feeling too tired to work. In overhearing some of the discussion, the Elder realized the young man was also a competitive dancer. His life was full of physical activity and, ironically, he wanted to move to California while he was still young and not ready to settle down. The Elder told him to go find a certain plant in the mountains and meditate for at least four hours. He was to sit on the edge of the mountain and see the pictures that the spirit people would show him. Then he was to share this when he brought the plant back. The young man was gone until the next morning. When he returned, he had a big smile on his face and holding a plant called a "Red Paint" or an "Indian Paint." The color of the plant was red, a message that it was time to stop, settle down, and meet a special person. I had already jumped to the conclusion that he was to find a pretty young girl and start a new life for himself. The Elder said, "Tsa-Yo-Gah (Jaybird), you cannot jump the rope if there is no rope there. Let him speak, before you jump to conclusions. He is struggling within himself, and he must allow these fears to come out to clear his way. You must guide him, not put more things in his path that create judgment." I suddenly realized that the turmoil was about a young man facing himself as a gay man and having to also face a family that might not be understanding or supportive. What a lesson I learned that day!

Native Americans understood the critical balance of the Universal Circle with Mother Earth, the animals, fish, birds,

plants, insects, and trees, and the ecosystem itself. All living
things were considered interdependent within the Universal
Circle. There was a true appreciation and respect for the
interdependence for life as everything existing in harmony
and balance. As an Elder said, "We are kin to all things, and
all things are kin to us . . . that's why we are the keepers of

Mother Earth and the protectors of all living things."

••••••••••••••••••••••••••••••••••••••••••••••••••••••••

## THE LIVING EARTH

Within the center of our Universal Circle is Mother Earth. She is considered alive and breathing, an organism with energy. As an Elder said, "Mother Earth is alive. She has the blood of rivers and streams carrying life-energy throughout her veins. Her heart is delicate and sensitive to the treatment and mistreatment by humans. She has fire inside of her, stronger than any woman today. When she hurts inside, she opens herself with such power and anger that her body shakes! It's not wise to upset her, but to dance for her and sing her songs that bring about calm. After all, she is the Mother of Life."

A British scientist, James Lovelock, has raised a rather controversial view—very similar to the Native American view—that the planet is a living organism, with the ability to regulate the global environment. His theory refers to life as interacting chemically and physically with the air, the waters, and the rocks to maintain optimum conditions. He named this organism "Gaia" (pronounced GUY-uh) after the earth goddess of the Greeks. The concept explains that Earth has evolved with tightly enclosed crustal rocks and oceans in a balanced atmosphere. Earth compensates for changes in the global climate by adjusting the rates at which gases such as oxygen, methane, and carbon dioxide are produced and removed from the atmosphere in a natural order. The effort to maintain harmony and balance can be upset by a meteor or asteroid impact and by human lack of respect and honor for protecting Earth. The real question is: Can we survive our own abuse of the very elements of life itself—water, air, earth, and the balance of all energy?

As an Elder said, "When we do harm to the Earth Mother, we do harm to ourselves." The same Elder says that we are also kin to the rocks as a fragment or part of ourselves. "It, too, [the rock] has energy of its own. We can communicate with the rocks, as they are keepers of energy. The precious ones, as we call them, have a special energy for particular reasons. . . ." He went on to talk about the crystals and other stones to be used for specific reasons defined in every culture of humans. His message during that lesson was for me to better appreciate and understand the value and respect for every rock and stone, and to know that the Earth Mother is a living organism. The few programs, activities, and money spent to recycle or to improve air or water quality are little compared to the waste and abuse of our natural resources. With many countries facing famine and new plagues and diseases, we realize the toll that eventually will be paid by all of us. We are all keepers of the physical environment, which in turn affects our physical being, health, and harmony.

........................................................

## THE PHYSICAL EVIDENCE

When I asked the Native American Elders about many of the recent scientific and archaeological discoveries, one of them said, "The ways of our people [Native Americans] were based on survival, so to understand us is to understand that we were located where there was food and water; it is that simple." My interest was in possibly finding out how long we were here in North America, and where we came from originally. He said, "That is easy. We did not come from any-where, we were here all along. They don't see any evidence because we didn't make any messes. We used everything we had and turned everything else back to the Earth Mother."

In recent years, there has been some interesting evidence of Native Americans being here in North America earlier than previously thought. As an example, molecular biologists examining remains buried in a Florida peat bog found a recognizable genetic message corresponding to a gene in humans. The DNA extracted may be able to link prehistoric people to living Indians. These digs in the Windover site near Titusville, Florida, include over 125 skeletons that are almost 8000 years old. It is amazing that the DNA would be so well preserved after all those years. Ironically, these people possibly had no tooth decay.

Another prehistoric site, Meadowcroft, is located near the Ohio River about 47 miles west of Pittsburgh. This appears to have been a Native American hunting camp around 20,000 years ago. This find indicated to archaeologists that the Woodland period spanned some 2500 years, beginning about 1115 B.C. There was maize and squash, staple foods of the Cherokee. There are some major finds to raise the eyebrows of scientists and archaeologists about the earlier Indian people. According to one Native American Elder, the recent finds at Meadowcroft and elsewhere are not by accident; people are now ready to better understand how earlier people were able to survive. As he put it, "We just need to go back to the real basics of life, before we don't have any life before us." He was really referring to better control of those things that pollute our environment, to living more basically, and being able to enjoy the natural world around us. He also talked about how families and clans used to come together to relax and to share stories and a meal.

........................................................

## THE LESSON OF THE EAGLE

There are certain animals, birds, and water beings that are referred to in Native American stories. Probably none of them have been as honored as the bald eagle. To Native Americans, it is considered as possibly the most sacred bird. The turtles of the sea and land also seem to have special significance in stories. The turtle is still considered as sacred by some Native Americans and referred to in their stories and ceremonies. Cherokee stories relate to the turtle as having a special purpose since the beginning of time. The turtle shells were worn by the Cherokee female dancers in earlier Green Corn ceremonies and today in Stomp Dances and powwows. The importance of the Eagle Dancers among the Cherokee and the use of eagle feathers by other Native Americans today attest to the honor given to the eagle.

The Eagle Dance among the Cherokee represents a strength and power to be honored. Unfortunately, while tens of thousands of eagles were once in North America, they are now rarely seen. The bald eagle was established as our national symbol in America by Act of Congress on June 20, 1782. It is the symbol of strength and freedom for America.

The eagle is a superb hunter with keen vision, similar to looking through a pair of six-power binoculars. Can you imagine it capturing a fish from a glide covering three miles of ocean? The needlelike claws are nearly two inches long and used like a vice, with tiny spikes on its toes to aid in holding slippery fish. It can weigh up to sixteen pounds with a seven-foot wingspan, and it may live as long as thirty years. Eagles mate for life and live totally devoted to their mates and their family. The family duties are fully shared by both male and female for guarding the nest or hunting for food. The eaglets are a wonder to behold as they spend about ten weeks in the large nests. They leave the family nest and soar away near the end of their first year. They will seek a mate in their fourth to sixth year when they develop the pure white head and tail of the adult bald eagle.

To me as a child, the eagle was a magical bird that could be seen swooping down with such elegance and strength of presence in the Great Smoky Mountains. While a 1940 law called the Bald Eagle Act strictly forbids killing, shooting, or capturing eagles, some people still seek the eagle for profit. Thanks to television shows like Mutual of Omaha's *Wild Kingdom*, many of us learned about these wonderful birds, even if not in real life. Among Native Americans, the eagle is considered sacred. The feathers are used in special ceremonies and for healing. There is thought to be a special energy in the feather, when skillfully used by Medicine Men or Women, that can detect energy changes in the body. As an Elder said, "Be careful how you use the eagle feather and know about where it came from. An eagle killed by gunshot would need to be cleared and blessed by a Medicine Man. Eagle feathers found are considered as a special gift to be used for healing and ceremony. The young person as an apprentice earns his or her feather with ceremony when ready to take on the challenge of the Medicine. You see, the eagle feather is no ordinary feather, it has special energy to be used only by those who know how to prepare the feather as taught by the keepers of the secrets." The lesson of the eagle came to me when I received my own eagle feather to become a helper for healing. Since this lesson is sacred, I am unable to share anything else about it, but I thought this much would help others to better appreciate the value of the eagle to Native Americans.

......................................................

## MEDICINE OF THE WEST

As there are lessons from the animals and birds, there are lessons from plants. As mentioned with the Natural Medicine of the South, there are helpers for our physical ills and wellness, as well as protectors from the plant spirits, that should be in our Medicine Bag. To understand the Medicine of the West, one must expand or open thought processes to reach an understanding about the wonderful gifts all around us that correct a deficiency or fill a void in our individual Medicine. These are gifts or helpers that focus on helping us rebalance, or to stay in balance, as we face the many stresses or physical threats each day. The Medicine of the West becomes our medicine shield as we go to battle each day. Some of these seem very ordinary, but can be powerful healers of the physical body.

**Alfalfa (Medicago sativa)**—Commonly found in the fields and fed to cattle, this small plant, which is about one foot tall with purple or blue flowers and coiled seed pods, is a must in your Medicine Bag. It is rich in calcium and nutritional value, and it was always welcomed in the Native American diet. It is considered good for lowering cholesterol and preventing atherosclerosis. The chlorophyll makes it good for fighting infections; it also contains vitamins A, B₁, B₆, B₁₂, C, and E and niacin. Rich in amino acids and protein, it is no wonder that animals enjoy this abundant food that is also a natural Medicine.

**Aloe (Aloe vera)**—Aloe is mentioned in this direction due to its special healing properties for the entire physical body. The tremendous overexposure we have to environmental pollution and toxins in our everyday life makes it necessary to seek these special healing plants. Aloe seems to produce an anti-aging effect on the skin and the polysaccharides in the aloe do not irritate the skin. Its ability to relieve inflammation and to penetrate the skin as an excellent emollient makes it a choice moisturizer. It is thought to help neutralize harmful foreign skin agents and enhance the removal of pathogens through the blood cells. It is also interesting that immune-stimulating herbs such as Purple Cone Flower have polysaccharides, like aloe vera.

**Blackberry (Rubus villosus)**—The common blackberries that folks are familiar with are also Cherokee Medicine. In the myths and stories, strawberries as well as blackberries have been used for special Medicine or qualities that bring people together, or cause something special or good to happen. Blackberries are used in a tea for settling the stomach, stimulating the system, and for relieving the pain of rheumatism. Blackberry tea is one of the favorite Cherokee remedies. The Medicine of the West includes trees, berries, and other fruits, as well as a lot of mixtures or formulas, for healing the entire body.

**Blue Cohosh (Caulophyllum thalictroides)**—This is another plant that has berries, and is deep blue in color. Cherokee women in earlier years used it for their menstrual cycle, possibly to regulate and for cramping. It was also used for colic with children. *Beware that the berries are really seeds that can be poisonous, and the plant can cause dermatitis on contact as it tends to irritate the skin.* I mention it here because it was one of the herbs called "Squaw Root" or "Papoose."

**Cabbage (Brassica oleracea)**—Fresh raw cabbage and cabbage cooked as a Cherokee form of sauerkraut are two of my favorite meals. While we did not know it contained histidine, as does broccoli, my mother and grandmother made sure it was in our meals to prevent cancer. We have used it for preventing cancer in the colon and rectum for many generations. It seems ironic that research is finally catching up to what my grandmother instinctively knew. We also knew that it would detoxify the system, but now we understand it has value in fighting the "bad" cholesterol (low-density lipoproteins). I still use raw juice from cabbage on occasion to cleanse my digestive system. As my grandmother would say, "You gotta' eat right to live right."

**Carrot (Daucus sativus)**—Carrots should be a part of everyone's daily snacks as freshly cut stalks of healthy habits. If an apple-a-day can keep the doctor away, then carrots-each-day will keep the Medicine person away. Carrots contain a natural antiseptic that is effective in the mouth, with the juice being effective for swelling and inflammation on the skin. It is good for lowering cholesterol and good before eating greasy foods. Also, the beta-carotene found in carrots is an anticancer nutrient. Since I tend to run low blood sugar, carrots are my energy booster snack. **Queen Anne's Lace (Daucus carota)** in the carrot family is used as a carminative and diuretic, particularly useful for gastrointestinal upset and heartburn. My grandmother would say, "You need carrots to *see* the beautiful young women." This is suggestive of the properties of vitamin A, known to improve night vision.

**Echinacea or Purple Cone Flower (Echinacea pallida)**—A medicine bag should not be without this herb. For many generations, echinacea has been used for headaches, stomach cramps, and sore throats, as well as for purification during traditional Native American sweats. The flowers are cone-shaped, with light purple and drooping petals, and are very popular among the Plains Indians as well as the Eastern Cherokee. Earlier, it was used as a cleansing agent to detoxify the body. I have seen it used successfully on skin infections and boils. Its recent popularity has been to enhance the body's resistance against infections, and for colds and the flu. Compounds using echinacea have been found to be antiviral and antibacterial, as well as immunostimulating due to the polysaccharides it contains. This might account for my grandmother giving me the herb along with fresh garlic for infections and severe colds. I would probably prefer to mix echinacea flowers in a quart of boiling water with equal teaspoons of burdock root powder and vitamin C, along with something to sweeten it a bit, and let it steep for about 15 minutes.

**Garlic (Allium sativum) and Onion (Allium cepa)—**
These are true healing gifts that can be used in fresh and
cooked foods each day. They are natural antibiotics, good
for headaches, sinus problems, hypertension, diabetic care,
lowering serum cholesterol, and just living a better quality of
life. My mother included them in just about everything
except dessert, and I am not sure we did not have garlic and
onion pie. America just has to eat more garlic and onion for
flavoring our foods and for good health.

**Hawthorn (Crataegus monogyna)—**This is a shrub or
tree that was used by the Cherokee, probably for increasing
circulation. A tea was used by the Cherokee ball players
before a competition to aid the players and to prevent
spasms. The use today is for the heart and for lowering blood
pressure. It is used as an antispasmodic and sedative in
herbal remedies.

**Horehound (Marrubium vulgare)—**This unusual-look-
ing plant with almost greyish-green leaves is found in pas-
tures and along roadsides. The flowers are small and have
two lips growing in whorls around the stems. It used to be
used as a laxative and as a remedy for snakebites. One time,
a Cherokee Elder was talking to me about his friend's dog living after a bad snake bite. The friend was upset, looking all
over for horehound and not being able to find it, because
someone had already picked all they could find to make
horehound candy. I asked where he found some. He replied,
"Well, I had some for my own use, but I did not want to share
it with an old dog. Guess I had to anyway; after all, he was my
friend."

**Peppermint (Mentha piperita)**—Already mentioned under "Mints" in the Medicines of the South, peppermint is considered very special by the Cherokee. As one Medicine Elder reminded me several times when learning about the herbs, the mints are here for folks to learn about for themselves. Peppermint is a plant that "talks to you, if you have a mind to listen." I have found it a good substitute for coffee, and I use it for headaches and just to calm my system. In the direction of the West, peppermint, as well as spearmint, is used to settle the stomach for good digestion and to calm the system after eating. I am having some peppermint tea as I write this book. You might want some while you read it, too!

**Oats (Avena sativa)**—Common oats or oatmeal are an often-overlooked Medicine. They are by far one of the least expensive forms of Medicine for the physical body that we could use. Oats are an antispasmodic, calming the nerves and stimulating the system. Generations of my family have eaten "oats-a-day" to keep us healthy, and used packs of oatmeal for aging skin and wrinkles. I mention it just so we do not overlook the value of certain foods for our Good Medicine.

**Pine tree (Pinus sylvestris, and others)**—Pine bark has been used by the Cherokee for many remedies. It is always used with other herbs to "give them strength," as one Elder put it. I am sure that in the future we will go back to the pine for many modern miracle drugs or remedies. The Cherokee feel that we are very closely connected in spirit to the pine. Its use during ceremonies when a person is passing on, to "rekindle the fire," still has much to teach us. As one Elder said, "The pines are all our brothers with special gifts of healing."

There is much to learn about our natural wonders in the form of plant and food helpers. I did not mention some commonly used herbs, fruits, trees, and foods used by the Cherokee in the Medicine Way, but there are foods that I do not want to ignore: beans and corn. As a Cherokee Elder put it, "Corn or 'se-lu' is our life, and don't forget the beans of life. They are our Good Medicine." Our physical health depends on harmony and balance in our lives. This balance is associated with what we do in our lives and how we do it. The story of the Redbird, which I will tell below, helps us understand that our harmony and balance are the center of all relations. We must remember that the plants are our helpers, but we must do some things to help ourselves in our relationships.

· · · · · · · · · · · · · · · · · · · · · · · · · · · · · · · · · · · · · · · · · · · · · · · · · · · · ·

## HOW THE REDBIRD GOT HIS COLOR

The balance of the West with the East is emphasized in the story of how the Redbird got his color. As an early Cherokee story goes, there was a little bird that wanted to be noticed and respected, like the Sacred Eagle. However, he was a little bird of earth-tone color, plain, and not easily seen by the others. If he was colored red, he thought, then he would be recognized by others for his power and beauty. Of course, he also wanted to be noticed by the female birds. He talked to one of the Elders in his clan council who told him he had to *earn* such a privilege. He explained that the color red was sacred, like the color black, and it had to be earned in a special way, through a vision.

Many moons went by without the vision to learn what he was to do to earn the red color. One day Raccoon and Wolf had a disagreement, which had something to do with Wolf always playing tricks on Raccoon. Of course, Raccoon really enjoyed playing with his friend, but he decided that he was tired of Wolf always getting the best of him. Knowing that Wolf was very quick, but also sometimes not so smart about things, he said, "Hey, Wolf, come chase me, I bet you can't catch me." Of course, Wolf replied, "Raccoon, I can always catch you, I'll even give you a running start." Raccoon ran as quickly as his little legs could take him to the water's edge, knowing that the water was very cold and that Wolf was afraid of the water's rapids.

Wolf took off with speed and agility to catch Raccoon. Raccoon scrambled as quickly as he could toward the water's edge, and grabbed onto a yellowroot plant and held on so as not to fall into the water. Of course, Wolf did not see him, thinking that Raccoon had jumped into the cold water. Wolf ran so hard that by the time he saw Raccoon, he was headed into the water's rapids. "Oh, this water is cold! Help me, Raccoon, you know I cannot swim!" Raccoon knew that he would be alright just floating down the rapids. Wolf clawed at the clay edge until he finally pulled himself out on to the clay bank. Being exhausted, he fell asleep in the warm sunshine. Raccoon quietly packed the soft red clay on Wolf's eyes, and it hardened in the warm sun.

The little bird was sitting on a small tree branch watching his friend play, when he heard Wolf cry, "I can't see, please help me! I can't see!" Well, the little bird went over to help Wolf. The little bird said, "I will help you, but you must promise to always play nice with Raccoon, and not to play tricks on your friends." Wolf exclaimed, "I promise, if I can just see again! I will also tell you where you can get a beautiful red color." The little bird pecked and pecked at the hard clay until Wolf could see again. Wolf told the little bird where to find a plant in the mountains called "Red Paint Brush," and with it the little bird painted himself red. To this day, Wolf plays fair with Raccoon, and I understand that the little bird is now called the cardinal or Redbird, clearly a bird of distinction.

The story provides us values to live by and lets us know that if we continue to seek and ask for something special, we may just receive it. Not all of us can be eagles, but we can have a kind nature or way about us in helping others, listening to others and trying to get along. Such stories, like our lessons in life, are to teach us respect, dignity, and how to be in harmony with all things in life, according to the Native American Elders.

·············································

## THE LESSON OF GRANDFATHER ROCK

The direction of the West has many physical lessons for us to learn for enduring life as a physical being. As the Rule of Opposites teaches us, listening to the spirit direction helps us balance our lives. As an Elder put it, "We should have learned the lessons taught by Grandfather Rock many generations ago." The Elder shared the story of a young boy who was concerned about his family being cold and hungry. This was at a time when there were many large animals, and people lived in damp caves in the Great Smoky Mountains. There are Cherokee that say it was near the highest mountain that we call Mount Mitchell, and others say it was near Clingman's Dome. The young boy would lie on one particular warm rock in the heat of the day and just look at the beautiful landscape where the sky would touch the mountains. One day, the young boy cried tears that dropped down upon the rock. "What can I do to help my family and the clan, there must be something I can do?" sobbed the boy.

As the boy fell asleep on the large rock in the mountains, he heard a gruff voice say, "I have heard you, and I can help you, if you will listen and learn." The young boy was startled! "Who is talking to me?" The voice continued, "I am the Grandfather Rock." The boy said, "How can you talk to me?" Grandfather Rock said, "I am part of your vision to seek answers, and you can hear me because you want to listen." He went on to share stories about how to start a fire by rubbing two sticks together over dried leaves. He taught the boy how to make a spear, ask the fish for food, and give thanks. He taught him a "Blessing Way" dance and song to show respect to all living things and to the Great One. "Ah-ho-e-yea-ha," the young boy sang his song and used the gourd rattle with small round rocks inside for a sound like the rushing water. He beat with a stick on the drum wrapped in animal skin to hear the sound of the heart. He used the bow and arrows to obtain skins and meat, using every part of the animal. And, of course, he always gave thanks. The family was happy, the animals were happy, and the plants would smile with their flowers. It was a good time for the young boy who was becoming a young man.

One day the young man went to the huge mountain and rested in the golden warm sunshine. As usual he heard the voice of the Grandfather Rock, "Well, it is time for you to go on your own. I have taught you all that is needed for you and your family, and for those to come after you. The boy said, "I cannot leave you now, I will be sad, I really need you!" Grandfather Rock said softly, "You are a young man now and eventually you will be the Medicine Man of your tribe. All you have to do to hear me is to close your eyes and open your spirit ears to the wind. This is your guide. Of course, you will always give thanks, seek to help others in using your gift, be humble, and respect the Elders, and now it is time for me to go." There was no other sound from the Grandfather Rock. However, to this day, every young boy and girl knows the wonderful gift of the rocks in the mountains where they can lie in the golden warm sun and may even hear a slight, gruff sound. It may be the wind, or it may be the Grandfather Rock.

The answer to our survival, today and tomorrow, is in relearning how to listen to the lessons of nature. After all, there may be a Grandfather Rock that may be able to share with us on how to live in harmony and balance with our environment.

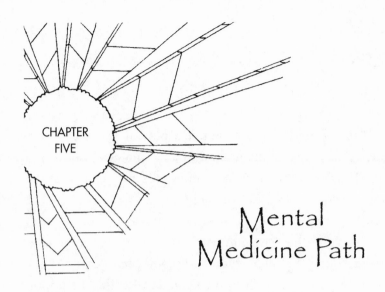

# Mental
# Medicine Path

The direction of the North is the mental path. This is the direction of learning and sharing. The color is usually white or blue, like the snow with the cold wind of the North. This direction usually includes the teachers and the creative minds that focus on some visionary activity to the point that they may prefer to work alone. The Medicine Elder asked me to "visualize the Smoky Mountains with their quiet and calm, with the coolness of a light breeze swirling around the huge bare rocks and lightly touching me like the spirits." He told me to breathe deeply, slowly, to "be in the place of calm" in my mind's eye, and then to travel to the garden where the flowers smile as they teach a new song. For me, it was a powerful learning experience. The purpose was to teach me to relax, but the lesson was about learning to take a "visionary look" at someone by understanding their spirit connection with the Universal Circle. This is all about "Mental Medicine."

..............................................................

## MENTAL MEDICINE

Mental Medicine is guarded as a sacred way or teaching by Native Americans. The mental aspect of a person is considered as being an integral part of the physical aspect of a person. Modern medicine is coming closer to the realization that the connections between physical and mental are more clearly definable than previously thought. The energy and influence of the environmental aspects are better understood today. I would rather applaud than criticize the progress made in modern medicine in realizing the importance of alternative and complementary medicine and therapies. In Mental Medicine, the use of biofeedback and relaxation techniques has been somewhat standardized and accepted by the medical communities. However, in the United Kingdom, the medical community has officially taken these techniques to an increased level of healing, by accepting that some people truly *do* have certain "helper" abilities to promote healing in their patients. From a Native American perspective, acceptance is the first rule to spiraling to a higher level of understanding.

The mental and physical are basically one in unity with the spirit self. Sometimes, we can get caught between the physical and the mental, just as the earlier stories told of some animals getting caught between the spirit and the physical worlds. This was very difficult for me to comprehend, except to understand that energy does not always travel neatly packaged as in a coaxial cable on a power line. In fact, the alternating currents as energy can travel distances outside the main power line in an alternating fashion. The mental energy is more elusive, in a sense, than physical energy that

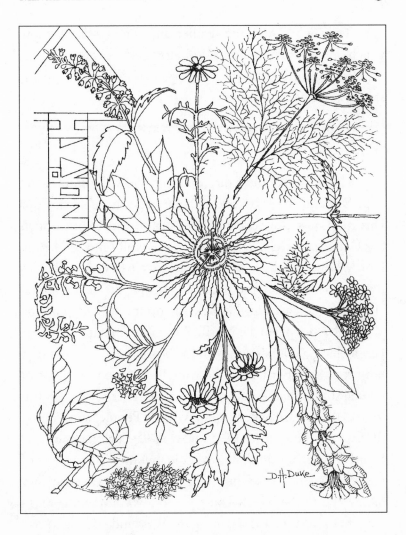

moves through a synapse process as our "electrical" system in the body. Sometimes these energies interfere with each other; as the Elder said, "They [these energies] tend to get all mixed up and throw the person out of balance. You gotta' know what's going on to not just jump in and think it is something spiritual going on. The best way to find that out is to help the person calm down, like taking a trip on the mountain. Then work with the feather and the crystal to know which one is which." Understanding the effect of energies on us, and the influences from others, is important in understanding the Mental Path.

........................................................

## THE "BEAR" TRUTH

The bear, like the wolf, tends to follow the spiral in all Four Directions. Of course, all animals go through the Four Directions just as we do, but they usually relate to one clan in the Universal Circle. The bear and the wolf tend to like the North; however, the bear likes to be a little lazy, according to the earlier stories. Some Bear Clan people are very cunning and prefer a "cave" in the West, as opposed to joining the Wind Clan people in the North. As an Elder put it, "The Bear People have a connection with the bear animals, in that they both tend to hibernate in the winter and don't like a lot of mental stuff. Oh, they like to play games, but they don't want to read the rules. They say to the Winged People, 'You stay up there, and I'll stay down here, and we will get along fine.' The Bear People really don't like the cold, but they like the heat of the South even less, so they wear their fur coats and say they have to go to the North 'cause it's too warm down here. In fact, they are better off staying in the West and coming to visit the Deer People in the North sometimes."

The lesson of the bear relates how the bear spirits volunteered to come down to the human world to help the human beings because they were so weak. As the story goes, there was a Bear Council to consider who among the bear spirits would give of their spirits to help the human beings. Black Bear said he should go down to teach the lessons of the

West, and White Bear said he would go down so the human being would learn the lessons of the North and join the Wind People.

When it was time, and the Thunder Beings came to guide the animals spirits to Mother Earth, the bear spirits were the last to leave, as usual. Some of the bear spirits got between the other animal and human spirits. Therefore, some humans are somewhat like bears and bears tend to be like humans in the physical form. As an Elder put it, "Have you ever seen a bear skinned? Well, it is just like a human man with claws. Of course, I have also seen some men that are just like bears in the way they walk, talk, and think. That's 'cause the bear was slow and got caught between the two worlds." This particular Elder was a female, and she taught me much about the female Medicine perspective. She also enjoyed joking about man being a lot like the bear.

The Mental Medicine teaches us that we have to understand all things in Nature to understand ourselves. You and I just have to listen and see how we relate to each thing in Nature. We do that by listening to the energy messages of the flower, the tree, the water, the rock, and everything we see in Nature. Of course, you may want to be subtle about talking to them; otherwise, someone might think you are mentally unbalanced. Actually, it is more mentally balancing to fit into the calm but active energy of Nature. One of the challenges is to find things on Mother Earth that can be "helpers" for us, to provide a sense of calm when we cannot be in the natural environment.

......................................................

## FIND YOUR OWN ROCK

Children, in a sense, are often our teachers. I often share with children that they can always find something in Nature that is special. As an exercise, I ask them to go with a parent or friend outside into a park or in a protected natural area to find a special little thing such as a leaf, a small rock, or a piece of wood that may have a special shape. Of course, I always have them leave something special with the Earth Mother, such as a piece of corn, to return thanks.

A small girl about five years old heard the story when I was a hospital administrator in Cherokee, North Carolina. She came into the hospital very excited one day, "Look! Look! I found this special rock. It's shaped like a heart!" She shyly leaned forward and handed me the rock, saying, "I brought it for you." I was so surprised that I stumbled in saying, "This, uh, is certainly a special rock. Thank you! And what did you leave for Mother Earth?" She was suddenly bright and cheerful, saying, "Oh, I told her you would take care of that!" We truly do learn from children. That experience was something special.

Each of us should find our own rock, too. As a matter of fact, how about doing that right now in this section of the book? While you are enjoying reading this, I want you to go outside and find a special rock. Listen carefully with touch and feel. If you are unable to go outside or do not have an "outside" to get to, then go in the calm of your mind to some special place and search for the special rock. Several years ago, "Rock Art" became very popular. Well, I do not want you to paint it, just keep it natural. Find a safe place to quietly relax—not while you are driving, please! Close your eyes and take a breath deeply, and slowly, a couple of times. Picture a place you have already been where there are rocks, possibly in the North. Visualize yourself finding a special rock. Note the size, shape, color differences, the feel, what kind it may be—and ask if it is alright for you to just keep it for a while. Now keep the rock in your hand and ask about its experiences and history, and see what comes into your mind as pictures. Are they still pictures or moving scenes? Now open your eyes and feel the sense of calm, knowing that you can feel that whenever you pick up the little rock. Be sure to put it in a special place. Say, "Wah Doh," which means thank you.

Sometimes we feel a sense of being alone and a sense of disconnection. The gift of a rock or a special stone is one of the oldest and best gifts to receive and to "give away." As counselors, teachers, parents, and friends, we can share with others the Native American teaching of finding something special. This is a Mental Medicine exercise that will be expanded in chapters 6 and 7 in discussions about crystals. It is important to know that these little gifts of rocks and stones provide energy sources that can calm and be helpers for healing. This is particularly true of people who feel or are going through "disconnect." It acts as a reminder that we have choices, and support, and can find something special if we seek it. It also teaches about caring, love, and healing while we, too, are connecting or reconnecting with someone or Nature. Of course, a flower's loving smile does the same thing. It is just that the rock lives forever, so it is a spirit energy that we can continue to hold on to at any time. That in itself is wonderful mental healing in the lessons of the North.

..........................................................

## RESPECT AND MENTAL HEALING

One of the first rules in Indian Medicine is RESPECT. This is the underlying basis to understanding Indian Medicine. This is also related to honor and humility. These are Mental Medicine actions that bring about interactions of the highest order in our lives. Unfortunately, many of us do not understand the power of these positive actions. These actions are helpers in maintaining or bringing about healing harmony in our lives. As an Elder said, "Teaching respect to the young ones for all things in Nature provides dignity for the person, clan, and tribe. Dignity is not an ego thing, but a spiritual thing." To learn about mental healing, we must first show respect for all things. Respect to everything in Nature teaches us one of the most powerful strengths we can have in our medicine bag, along with respect for our connection with Nature.

The traditional Indian practitioner is concerned with the person's relationship with everything in the environment. This relationship must be "looked at" first before deciding on the healing ceremony, in a traditional sense. In our modern medical setting, we expect to get some type of medicine or pharmaceutical treatment that is going to take away whatever is the problem. The same expectation would not exist with the traditional Indian going to a traditional practitioner. First, there is no expectation, only thanks for the gift. The traditional view is based more on an illness being the result of imbalance and disharmony or "dis-ease," rather than "disease." Instead of "expect," we need to "respect."

The healing is somewhat a secondary result from the primary choices that an individual person must make to bring about harmony of the energies. It may be as simple as going to the creek bank for a certain ceremony or as complex as experiencing a "sweat" in a traditional sweat lodge with several days of ceremony and vision seeking. This form of "Energy Medicine" is intended to bring about openness for the helpers to promote the healing; however, the choice must still be made by the individual, family, and clan in the Native American Way. As with modern medicine, there are different specialists for various imbalances in Indian Medicine.

As individuals respect and accept the helpers and the healing choices they have made, they will also accept their own growth and lessons from the "dis-ease" experience. Is it physical or mental, or does it make any difference? As the Elder said, "We should focus on the choices we made for healing and not on the helpers there to guide us. It is not about what someone gives to you, but what you give away, the respect you demonstrate, and the opening up you do to Good Medicine choices that bring about healing; we are just helpers. Respect that, and you will learn the lesson of Mental Healing."

...............................................................

## THE DEER AND THE BEAR

A French philosopher by the name of Descartes managed to encourage the separation of the human into a mind and a body. The mind and body relationships are one in the traditional view of Indian Medicine. An Elder explained this relationship to me this way, "The deer is a cunning animal, considered sacred, because it is the mind of the universe. It hears and sees all things, and you can talk to the deer. The bear, on the other hand, likes to sleep and eat when hungry. The bear is the body of the universe, just doing what comes naturally, without regard to anything or anybody, except for the messages received. Each cell of the body has the messages and memory of all time. We can condition our bodies to listen and to receive those messages as the sacred deer does for Mental Healing."

A simple exercise is to sit on a mountain, or an imaginary one in your vision. Take a couple of deep breaths and "see" what you feel. Where are the muscles tight? Where do you feel any pain, and how is your heart beating? Ask any questions that come to your mind. Just realize how you can really talk to your body and have it respond. Sense Nature and the sounds around you, and just note how your senses can become heightened or relaxed to receive or cut out things. The body and the mind can relax and come into balance as you focus on your center or spirit self. We are an integral part of the universe and natural world around us. Learn to just "be" in any environment, wherever you are. If we learn to listen well, we can hear messages from those we are close to and even those who are no longer with us. As one Elder put it, "It is wonderful to just be alone, because we then learn just how not alone we really are. . . ." In that moment of silence, we probably come closer together with everything!

························································

## INTEGRATED HEALING

Modern medicine has been dominated by views surrounding the old "germ" theory. In earlier years, we conquered diphtheria, malaria, and smallpox by advanced medicines and environmental controls. The uses of antibiotics for pneumonia and meningitis to cure these deadly conditions were miracles. Today we transplant hearts and kidneys, and there is no telling where we will go in the future. However, we still cannot control the common cold, except to provide remedies or temporary relief. We face the deadly virus that causes AIDS. We have touched on one of those ancient teachings today in research with psychobiological and psychoimmuniological aspects or how the mind associates with the body and the immune system. At least we are now more accepting of the human as a total system with pathogenic and regenerative forces at work.

Modern medicine is coming closer to the Native American traditional beliefs and the Eastern Indian (from India) beliefs on different ways to view the body and mind. Traditional views focus on concepts of restoring the system by bringing it back into harmony and balance; functioning at some level with balance and intervention; and dealing with harmony and balance as requiring prayers and Blessing Ways for passing-over, which is the death of the physical. As an Elder said, "The individual heals, and we are the helpers in that process or experience; but sometimes prayers are required to open the doors to healing."

......................................................

## THE PATH OF MENTAL HEALING

The concerns of today with suicide, homicide, depression, and "mental illness" relate to stresses and things we have learned or not learned. There are no easy answers to abuse and harm done by people. We get caught in this dilemma of provincial thinking about protecting our communities by keeping the abusers and criminals out while still being our brother's keeper. On a trip with several Medicine Men and Women to the mountains for a ceremony, I asked them what to do about a young girl who was raped by a man twice her age with a record of repeated crime. A quick response was, "Drop him off the mountain. If the crime was this bad, then he has lost his spirit. There is no time to learn respect when you have just shown disrespect. Teach the young people the traditional stories and values, but do not allow harm and abuse of the spirit! Drop him off the mountain, so at least his spirit, if he has one, can fly." While the offender could be punished and the offended could heal, the act of rape, like murder, could not be corrected in this physical life. The spirit void would remain there in this life.

Another path of healing is Nature's Medicine. With so much stress to succeed and to get ahead, our young people are experiencing increased depression and disharmony. Many good medicines have been learned from the Native American gifts from Nature. It has been estimated that some 36 million Americans suffer from mood disorders. While I encourage use of our current medical treatments, I personally prefer more natural ways of reducing stress, such as changing some things in our lives; choosing new paths; making new friends and dropping some old ones that create "overstress"; reducing overloads; joining support circles; and following therapies that are helpers to healing. An Elder said, "There is no one answer or remedy to this thing you call 'mental.' It is also physical, spiritual, and natural. Fear is the biggest problem. Find the fear, and then find a new path."

It is important here, I believe, to mention that the mental illness and mental conditions that were considered "hush-

hush" in years past can now be shown as mental disorders of a biological nature, perhaps in brain chemistry or structure. The advances in neuroscience have been tremendous in the past few years. Our understanding of chemical neurotransmitters today allows for ways to regulate moods and disorders. This also means that there are more medicines that can be "helpers" to rebalance our mental-physical activity, along with behavioral therapies and alternative techniques and methods. The key is integrated healing approaches using modern and alternative and complementary therapies.

......................................................

## INTEGRATED HEALING OF TOMORROW

The modern medicine of today and tomorrow is integrated, using many alternative therapies as helpers for choices leading to harmony and balance. The stresses of today can be "calmed" by psychobioimmunological therapies to direct "killer" or "T-cells" to control the out-of-control cancers of tomorrow. These therapies allow mind-body therapies to retrofit and rebalance energies and heal the "spirit." Early Native Americans learned techniques and approaches that we have to relearn to relieve stresses in our complex world. Our perceptions and our beliefs will be used in the modern medicine of tomorrow as a form of integrative energy therapies. The concept of "treatment" is fairly obsolete, even today, in an environment of so many choices. Energy Medicine does allow for many therapies to promote healing, rather than a single therapy. We are living in an exciting time due to the tremendous advances that will be taking place in our modern medicine in the near future. Mental Medicine will be advanced by magna-energy therapies and energy balancing, as we accept some new trial therapies of tomorrow.

The depression of today will be the "expressed suppression of fear" therapies in the next few years with a focus on helpers to assist in building renewal paths from harmful friendships, marriages, abuse, and harmful environments. Chemical imbalances associated with depression, and middle-age crises will be treated by techniques that will allow for interaction and integration of therapies to find the new direction of choice for each person. The mental and physical will be integrated with the spiritual and natural aspects of a person for balance and harmony. In essence, the Four Directions will be integrated into modern medicine and health preventions, just as Indian herbs and remedies were borrowed and included into the drugs and treatments of today. Hopefully, this time the Native Americans will be thanked and appreciated for their contributions.

We will learn to trust ourselves rather than taking on the criticism of others who are projecting their own will on us. Listening to the Native American stories and teachings can be an excellent learning exercise. We might well establish "rebalancing" centers for the future with a variety of modern and alternative approaches within one building. An exciting therapy will be "Emerging Therapies," such as the ones used in Indian Medicine for learning to talk to and listen to the spirit self for healing to emerge from within. As people have learned self-hypnosis, some old teachings will provide some new ways to use outside energy helpers such as plants, trees, and those from the mineral-rock clans to learn balancing of energies.

We can relearn the Native American teachings of the past and apply them to our world tomorrow to better integrate, rather than segregate, our lives. Our modern medicine of today can be integrated with the wonderful Natural or Energy Medicine of tomorrow. The answer is the traditional teaching of acceptance, showing respect, and allowing dignity without criticism of anyone or any approach used that causes no harm and allows for healing within the person, including the family and the environment.

•••••••••••••••••••••••••••••••••••••••••••••••••••••

## THE MENTAL RULE OF OPPOSITES

The essence of "being" in today's world of stresses is to be able to let down a little bit by being ill. However, the emphasis seems to be focused on "doing" and not in "being"—unless the reference is to "being somebody." People who spend too much time in the cold-and-alone North, so to speak, or who spend too much time in studying, should go to the direction of the South. The Rule of Opposites would indicate playing in the ocean or feeling the sense of freedom of a child. The objective would be to relax and release through playful activities with others or with a favorite person or animal—and to have fun in the Direction of the Natural.

•••••••••••••••••••••••••••••••••••••••••••••••••••••

## CROSS-OVER EXERCISE

The Medicine Men and Women taught me a way to get out of a rut or to cross over from one direction to another. A "Cross-Over" exercise is a way of getting out of an energy rut or a comfort zone that requires the shifting of mental energy.

Find (or visualize) a stream of water that can be crossed by walking over a bridge. It is important to touch the water, and even rub some of the water on your forehead. Be sure it is a clean stream in Nature. Give thanks to the water and say to yourself or out loud that you are going to experience Cross-Over so as to move yourself in the direction of healing. (The bridge can be visualized mentally, if you are unable to physically go to a Cross-Over location in a natural environment.) Slowly walk across the bridge while looking ahead, rather than down at the water, with your eyes slightly opened to be sure you are walking safely. "Feel" the sense of energy movement as you continue to move slowly. If someone is crossing in front of or behind you, just stop and let this person pass. Continue to move across until you feel a sense of calm. Once you feel the sense of calm, then "feel" which is more comfortable: looking up the stream, or looking down the stream? Where are you on the bridge?

Then continue slowly across to the other side. Once you have crossed, explore your feelings. Go ahead and write down what you feel, so you can look at it later. The messages will tell you the direction with which you are connected. Sometimes you get very subtle messages, or a picture of something that may not fit until you think about it some more. If you are in the middle of the bridge when you feel the sense of calm, then you are alright being with others and allowing the energy to go around you. If you are at the starting side, then you may not be ready for change. If you feel the sense of calm at the other side, then your spirit has already made the change and may be waiting for you. Looking up the stream refers to being actively involved, and looking down stream means you are probably ready to disengage a little now, or maybe you can just follow rather than leading. The exercise is designed to set up opposite energies, with water being a powerful energy for "clearing." While a fun exercise, Cross-Over is also very revealing for "shifting" you to another direction.

Many of the following herbs or plants as helpers can also be used to rebalance and shift your energy, and to enhance the immune system or facilitate action for healing.

........................................................

## MEDICINE OF THE NORTH

The Medicine of the North is for calming the spirit, learning how your body acts and reacts, and releasing the stresses of life. The focus is on learning and sharing the wisdom of the Medicine within all of us.

**Catnip (Nepeta cataria)**—Catnip is a member of the mint family, with hairy-like branches that grow about five feet high with oblong and pointed leaves. The color of the flower matches the color of the North direction—white with purple specks. It blooms in the summer-to-fall months. Deep blue or purple is the color for the North, but some Elders refer to the North as the "land of the white" where people have purple hearts and require calming Medicines because they are so intense. The leaves are crushed and used as a poultice to relieve pain. The tea is made by bringing two cups of water to a boil; add one teaspoon of cut herb, and let it steep for about fifteen minutes. My grandmother called it "nip tea" and used it, usually at bedtime, for calming under stressful times.

**Chamomile (Matricaria chamomilla or recutita)**—My grandmother referred to this as a "blessing herb;" her mother told her that it was shared with the Cherokee when a white man who was very sick and spoke a strange tongue came to them for help. His gift for the Medicine help was a beautiful plant that grew about a foot tall with pale green leaves and white flowers and that was good for headaches and calming the body. The tea is made by steeping about two teaspoons of dried flowers for about twenty minutes or so in a pint of boiling water. It can also be used as a skin wash for rashes.

**Fennel (Foeniculum vulgare)**—My grandmother would say that fennel would "dance in the wind, and show off with its lacy look" and "be a seed that would make you kissable." It grows about five feet tall with small yellow flowers in umbrella-like clusters. Its seeds are used in flavoring fish dishes, and a tea from the seeds was popular for indigestion and cramps. A tea of fennel with an equal amount of peppermint leaves is good to calm an overactive system.

**Feverfew (Tanacetum parthenium)**—This plant is used for headaches and as an antimigraine agent, probably due to an active substance called parthenolide in the plant leaves. Because of the content being so small (less than 0.1 percent) in plants found in America, it is better to purchase the dried leaves at 0.2 percent or greater. This is one of those plants that can require someone specialized in natural medicines and their uses, particularly since there can be some side effects such as lightheadedness. It does seem to be good for arthritis and for anti-inflammatory uses. The early Cherokee used "fever root," sometimes today called coral root or crawley root (*Corallorhiza orontorhiza*), from the orchid family, as a mild sedative and in treating fevers and arthritis. This is similar to the use of feverfew.

**Peppermint (Mentha piperita) and Spearmint (Mentha spicata)**—While used mostly as antiviral agents and for the physical ailments of an upset stomach, these mints are also used for calming nerves and for relieving headaches. They are in the Cherokee formulas along with other herbs to calm the action of some stronger herbs that might stimulate the stomach. I just like to put a mint leaf in my regular tea.

**Mullein (Verbascum thapsus)**—This plant is commonly found along the roadsides growing about eight feet high with a rosette of leaves and a tall spike of yellow flowers. The large concentrations of mucilage in mullein make it a substance that soothes the mucous membranes. When made into a tea, it can be useful for respiratory ailments. I would advise seeking advice on mixtures from an herbalist. It can also be used for anti-inflammatory purposes and for those nagging rheumatism pains. As a Medicine of the North, it is excellent for nervous conditions, and is also rich in minerals. Some feel mullein can be narcotic, but I have not found it to be harmful. I recommend caution with this plant, however, because its hairy and soft leaves are excellent places for bugs and other smaller varmints to nest.

**Passion Flower (Passiflora incarnata)**—This is a true Medicine of the North with the white flowers with purple, deep blue, or pink crown blooms growing on a vine some twenty-five feet in height. Its use in earlier years was as a seda-

tive or for nervous conditions and hysteria. I would not recommend trying to make your own preparation. The flower
top, leaves, and roots were used for heart conditions and
muscle spasms and muscle conditions, particularly with the
eyes, in earlier years. An Elder once told me to get the young
"woman of my eye" some passion flowers; then she would
have something to settle her nerves when I "lit her fire." Well,
I was too humble and I settled for an unknown flower in the
field that better described my shyness.

**Skullcap (Scutellaria lateriflora)**—Skullcap was considered a plant that a dog might have eaten when running loose
and acting mad or out of control. This was one of the plants
considered for female Medicine to promote menstruation,
but commonly used as a strong sedative. It is used as an
herbal remedy for lowering cholesterol and in arthritis relief.
Here again, this is a plant that must be prepared by someone
who is very familiar with it and its potency.

**Valerian (Valeriana officialis)**—This is one of my
choices for use as a natural relaxant. It is used for back problems where there is frequent pain and for migraine headaches. It was used by early Cherokee as a healing herb due to
the antispasmodic properties in "quieting the nerves, so the
body could heal." I have heard that it attracts earthworms, so
"keepers of the planting spots" would plant a border of valerian around the area to attract worms to till the soil naturally.
I would recommend purchasing this one with instructions
on its use.

**Yarrow (Achillea millefolium)**—My grandmother said that her mother as an "herb doctor" used yarrow for folks that had inflammation in joints, and for the edema associated with gout. It was also a "female Medicine," but she said that was none of my business. I do know that a mixture of yarrow tea and chamomile as found in herbal remedies can be effective on sore nipples and skin that is chapped by weather, which was very common years ago. The yarrow flowers, as well as the rest of the plant, can be used in a chicken soup remedy for colds and fevers, as an Elder said, "to purify the system of toxins." A tea of yarrow is made by boiling a pint of water with an ounce of dried yarrow leaves.

**Wild Cherry (Prunus serotina)**—Wild cherry is well known for colds and sore throats. The Cherokee also used it for lung conditions, to calm the stomach, and for sores. The Wild Cherry Bark was a tonic; it does have a volatile oil that aids digestion and can act as a mild sedative. This is probably the reason that folks with heart conditions were encouraged to put some bark in their tea and sip it at night.

There was always a Cherokee Elder who would allude to something special that was male or female in the Medicine of the North. The connection of the North and the South was always considered by early Cherokee as very special and tantalizing to a person's spirit. There is a story that I want to share that might help explain this special Medicine effect.

·········································································

## THE NORTH'S BRIDE FROM THE SOUTH

Among the many stories of the Cherokee is one that tells of the attracting and repelling of energies of the opposite directions. The North decided to take a trip, so he thought of going to the South. He had fun in the warm direction and met the daughter of the South. She was so beautiful that he wanted to marry her and take her to his home. The South was not pleased with the North coming so far South, because he was too cold. The South told his daughter that she would have to go back with the North, because he could not be allowed to stay very long in the South, or otherwise the South would freeze. Well, she agreed to go home with him to the ice houses and Ice People.

After a few days, the ice houses started to melt, and the Ice People were sweating. The Ice People called for council with the North to let him know that his beautiful bride would have to return to the South; otherwise, in time, the entire North would eventually melt away. While sad, the North knew the council was right; but days would pass as the North became hotter. The council met again and said, "She is the daughter of the South, she must return to where she grew up. Her nature is warm, and that is where she belongs, in the South." Well, the North was very sad, but he sent her home to her family in the South. To this day, the North sneaks a brief trip toward the South to briefly touch his beautiful bride living in the South. I also heard that she sometimes sneaks a trip toward the North, but only long enough to not melt the Ice People and their houses. They are always glad to see the North smile with sunshine, but only for a short time.

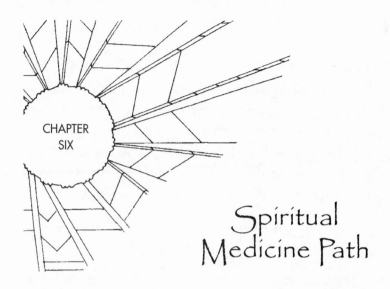

# Spiritual
# Medicine Path

The direction of the East is the Path of the Spiritual. The color associated with the East is Red. In Cherokee stories, the "Red Thunder Beings" would travel the spirit path to and from the skyvault through the direction of the East. Spirit beings that are coming into the physical world for birth would travel from the skyvault through the center of the Universal Circle into the East. Through the East, the spirit beings would travel for "clearing" to the direction of the South for birth into the physical world. This was a very sensitive subject in the teachings, and I had to be able to separate traditional teachings from the influence of religious teachings. While there were many parallels, the stories in the Cherokee language used distinctive words that could be interpreted as similar to religious teachings of various influences. It is my intent to present the traditional and to leave the interpretation and similarity to any other teachings to you.

The term "spiritual" in reference to the direction of the

East means a way of life based on the "spirit" influence. The earliest teachings I could find related to the spirit as being like the Eagle, who represents the "spirit core" within us all. Our center or fire with the "spirit cord" connects us to the Great One in the skyvault. Therefore, we always give thanks and give offerings to the fire in the form of a special tobacco mixture and corn meal to carry a message to the Great One.

## THE SACRED FIRE

The Cherokee story of the Sacred Fire starts with the beginning of our spirits coming to the Earth Mother. The Cherokee were the ancient mountain people of the East who were told to go to the South as children of the Great One. They were told by the Star People that they would always be connected to the stars for direction and for understanding that their connection was with the Universal Circle. As a continuous reminder, they would lay a circle of stones on the Earth Mother and build a fire in the center.

Anytime the people would gather around the sacred fire, the wind would be evoked with a special wood. The Star People would be watching, and the smoke of the fire would carry messages from the people. The Eagle's wing would fan the fire for strength, and the people would dance and sing to the Four Directions around the circle. Even if there was not an actual fire, as long as people were in the circle, the spirit of the fire would be there.

The special firewood would always include the cedar (the cedar log would also be the beginning of the mound or longhouse). The firekeeper would keep the fire alive with woods that would give of themselves, including the fire-

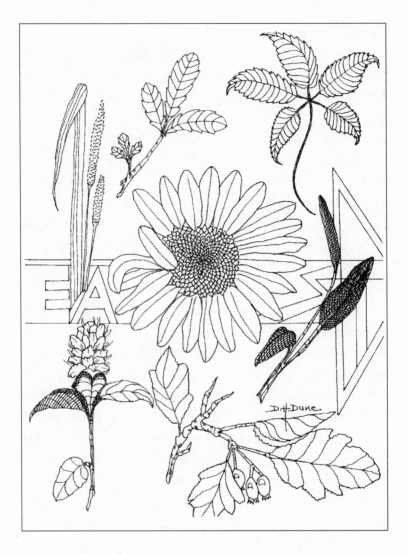

maker weed or fleabane. Only at the Green Corn ceremony would the earth be moved away from the cedar log or post and the Four Directions cleared for the sacred ground. No one would walk on this ground until they were "cleared" or smudged with the smoke of the special tobacco that only a few would know how to prepare. This was the beginning of the Sacred Fire.

A new fire would be started by rubbing two pieces of wood together with golden rod and the ashes of the First Fire. This would be the beginning of the spring ceremony. Each spring, the families and clans would clean their hearths and kindle new fires from the new-fire ceremony. While the original sacred fire, or the Eternal Flame, was taken on the Trail of Tears from the East to the place now called Oklahoma in the autumn of 1838, the fire is now shared between the Eastern Band of Cherokee Indians and the Cherokee Nation in Oklahoma. Each year, a ceremony is held to honor the Sacred Fire and the traditions of a people who always kept the fire and the cultural traditions alive.

As I was learning which woods to use and how to mix the special tobacco in the autumn of 1960, an Elder said, "It is up to us to teach the old ways to keep the fire inside our people alive. The Sacred Fire inside of us must not be from the fire of hate or revenge, but from the Good Medicine that lights our inner self and enlightens others as we share the teachings. Otherwise, we will be no better than those who attempted to dominate and manipulate us." The fire repre-sents the East and the doorway to the center or "core self" within each of us, as our connection with the universe.

∙∙∙∙∙∙∙∙∙∙∙∙∙∙∙∙∙∙∙∙∙∙∙∙∙∙∙∙∙∙∙∙∙∙∙∙∙∙∙∙∙∙∙∙∙∙∙∙∙∙∙∙∙∙∙∙∙∙

## SPIRIT OR SPIRITUAL

The term "spiritual" has a broad meaning in the Native American culture. The term "spirit" in Indian Medicine refers to an active and alive flow of energy that connects us all to the Universal Spirit. The term "spiritual" refers to a way or teaching, similar to a path or belief that we hold in our values.

Sometimes used to mean the same thing, the words "spirit" and "spiritual" can be used or referred to differently in ceremonies and in the old teachings. Both are unlike the meaning associated with religion, and both can be interchanged with a person's religious belief or choice of religious activity. This is one of the reasons that Indian people were alright with accepting different religious beliefs. The Spiritual path was never taken away from the Native American people; the cultural traditions and ancient teachings of an original people are still with us today.

Indian Medicine has taken on the concept of good and bad in terms of "Good Medicine" referring to helping others, herbal remedies, ceremonies, and other "helper" activities. The old teachings refer to conjuring as neither good nor bad. It is simply an action or activity to change or interfere with something going on with a person. This is one area of Indian Medicine that does need to be clarified. Conjuring can be divination or an action to cause another action. As an example, Medicine Elders using a crystal on a string to find something lost is a form of conjuring, in a sense. Ceremony or an action related to the spirit world to break an interference that is occurring with someone is a form of conjuring. It does not mean it is bad, unless it is intended to harm. Every Medicine Elder will tell you that such actions can "mirror" or come back on a person.

No one wants to have some negative action mirror back on them, unless he or she is trying to cause self-harm. However, people do this every day in life. As an example, smoking with the understanding that it can cause you cancer and lung disease or illness is taking a risk. A young person drinking or taking drugs is usually taking an informed risk.

This can be the same as conjuring; the only difference is that one is doing it to oneself, rather than to someone else. If a person sells a drug or gets a young person hooked on drugs, that is conjuring, in a traditional sense. The user may be very informed or afraid, but is "conjured" into believing that it will be fun or will take him or her to a special place. The mirror-back will be the harm it does to the person's body. Therefore, the "spirit" of something must be good or a helper that is positive, rather than misrepresenting the "spiritual" meaning of the action.

......................................................

## MEDICINE OF THE EAST

The Medicine for the Spiritual Direction is associated with fire, which brings together everything in harmony and balance, bonding, and cleansing or purifying. It is usually associated with the heart and the circulatory system. While much of this Medicine has been lost over the generations, Cherokee today have a "sense" of how important it still is to approach the plants, circle around them, and only pick one if there are four or more. At first, it was surprising to me in learning about these herbs that some very simple and commonly found herbs would have such power in healing. As one Elder said, "These are all 'wonder plants' as special helpers for the healing to take place."

**Alfalfa (Medicago sativa)**—Alfalfa is mentioned again in the Direction of the East as a supplement for balancing the body, mind, and spirit. In our world of stressful living where we're always in a hurry, we really require supplements such as vitamins, minerals, and herbal preparations. According to the Medicine Elders, alfalfa is a gift we learned from the ani-mals. Get the alfalfa in tablet form and take a couple before each meal. This is particularly true when eating processed and cooked foods where the enzymes are destroyed. Alfalfa is good for enzyme content and for vitamin A, which is becoming so important in preventing damage to the skin due to environmental overexposures. Protection of your skin, as well as the mucous membranes of your throat, nose, and intestines, can be improved and protected by vitamin A. Alfalfa contains several enzymes that aid in digestion of pro-teins and conversion of starches and sugars. Alfalfa is men-tioned in the East as a special gift for all the family and for balancing other herbal helpers.

**Dock or Yellow Dock (Rumex cripus)**—Sometimes called "Curly Dock" by the Cherokee who would gather it in the spring along with other young plant leaves for salad greens. The "spring salad" was a tonic that Native Americans and settlers alike would appreciate and share. It is also a nat-ural form of laxative, cleansing for the system. Similiar to sar-saparilla, it was intended to be a sping tonic to take care of the winter sluggishness. It is high in vitamin C and iron. The yellow could be used as a dye, and the Cherokee would use it for itch and put crushed leaves on sores. The mixture is about a handful of fresh or dried root in a quart of boiling water, steeped for about fifteen minutes. Of course, there are other herbs that mix well with this for cleansing and purify-ing, such as sage.

**Ginseng (Panax quinquefolium)**—Our "five-fingered friend," as an Elder called it, has always been a healing tonic for building our systems for health and immunity. It was considered by the Cherokee as a male-female herb with healing effects for both. My grandmother called it the "jump-start herb." It can be used for many purposes, including for headaches, nervous conditions, and vertigo; and the root can be mashed and applied to stop bleeding. When she was close to passing on at over ninety years old, I asked her about ginseng. She said it was good for stimulating the systems of older folks for eating and for better absorption of vitamins and minerals, and excellent for diabetics. As she put it, "You don't have to be a doctor to know that the plants know better than we do. Sometimes the Elders know better than their doctors what they need. Ginseng is a gift."

**Heal-all or Self-heal (Prunella vulgaris)**—The early Cherokee had many healing uses for this plant that was said to have a special name, "Ga-ni-qui-li-s-ki." Most plants were given common names that were associated with their use, but a few had special "healing" names. From the mint family, this plant with deep-purple clusters of flowers at the top of the stem can be recognized in fields where there is some dampness. Heal-all reproduces with runners as well as by seeds. It was used for bruises, burns, sores, cuts, and many other external purposes. Internally it was used as a calming agent, as a gargle, and as a remedy for treating diarrhea. While I am personally not comfortable in recommending internal use, I mention it here because of its sacredness to many Native Americans.

**Hawthorn (Crataegus oxyacantha)**—While the berries have been used to treat the heart and blood pressure as a natural herb, herbalists have also used it as a vasodilator to relax the blood vessels. It is also considered good for inflammation of the heart and for stressful working conditions that put the heart at risk. Its use as a producer of natural adrenalin has also been recorded. The leaves are used as a cardiac depressant to slow the heartbeat. *However, use it under the care of a specialist or naturopath who understands how to control its use.* Otherwise, it could be risky to try using on your own.

**Sage (Salvia officinalis)**—The Native American use of sage is varied. It is considered sacred among some tribes. The Cherokee used a tea of sage leaves for a sore throat; congestion in the lungs; colds; nervous conditions; asthma; bowel problems; "female weakness;" and in many other formulas or remedies. To make a tea, use about two teaspoons of dried or fresh leaves steeped in two cups of boiling water. This can also be used for a common cold and as a wash for sores and skin problems. I have heard of it being used for those folks that sweat excessively, by mixing it with equal parts of dried hops and stinging nettle. An Elder mentioned its use with heart problems that he had learned from a Sioux Medicine Man. Like others in the Direction of the East, sage is one of those "cure-all" herbs.

**Sunflower (Helianthus annuus)**—This is one of the sacred herbs used by the Cherokee and mentioned in stories and myths passed down for many generations. It was used as a folk remedy for rheumatism and similiar pains, as well as for respiratory conditions. I have also heard of it being used for sunstroke with other substances. The diuretic and expectorant properties may be the reason for its importance as a pulmonary remedy. The seeds were used as a food, having about 25 percent protein, with rich amounts of vitamins, such as A and B-complex, and of minerals such as calcium and magnesium. While precautions have been suggested, I would say to just check with the natural-food stores and herbalists. Sunflowers used to be commonly seen lining the "planting spots" of Cherokee food gardens. As an Elder said, "The sunflower is more than an herb, it is a spirit-healer, gifted by the Great One, chosen for its special healing ability. We will one day learn what the old ones already knew about this special plant and seed."

Sometimes a plant with its special properties also had the ability to send a prayer to the Great One in some special way that we do not know or remember today. The sunflower is one of those sacred plants, like Indian tobacco and sage, with the ability to aid us in prayer as a messenger to the Great One.

. . . . . . . . . . . . . . . . . . . . . . . . . . . . . . . . . . . . . . . . . . . . . . . . .

## PRAYER/PRAYER CHANTS

Prayer is an active process in the Native American traditional and cultural way of life. It is often in the form of prayer chants and ceremonial activities. It is very common in the teachings and stories that refer to giving thanks each day for the rising Sun and for the healing of all things. Prayers were generally not used to ask for anything but guidance and to give thanks. This is usually expressed in a Blessing Way as an active prayer process.

The process of praying for Native Americans is fairly open, but subtle; we use certain hand movements, such as passing a hand over the food before partaking of a meal. An open palm may mean "thank you" as a gesture, and the open—or even closed—palm pointing toward Mother Earth is also a sign of thanks. The same is true with pointing the open palm(s) toward the sky in ceremonies, which signifies giving thanks to the Universal Spirit and the Great One. As a subtle way to pray or open the energy, this can be powerful in sending a message.

A message or prayer may be sent by offering some tobacco or a similar mixture of plants and tree barks to a fire during ceremonial times. These things are mentioned so that nonIndians can better appreciate the sacredness of this process as prayer.

There are some good references in the library and the book stores. I was particularly struck by a book written by a physician, Larry Dossey, M.D., called *Healing Words: The Power of Prayer and the Practice of Medicine* (Harper/ San Francisco, 1993). While co-chairing a panel on "Mind-Body Interventions" at the Office of Alternative Medicine at the National Institutes of Health, he became convinced of prayer in the healing process. His evidence is based on case studies and provides insight into what Native Americans would not challenge—that prayer is as integral a part of the healing process as medical treatment. In some cases, prayer as a spirit healing process was the difference that helped the person to live. Prayer is a spiritual connection. As the Elder said, "It is our way to accept, and it is important that we all accept prayer as an active spirit energy."

Native American ceremonies include prayer-chants to heal the Earth Mother and to bring harmony to the universe. For some who have difficulty with saying the word "prayer," maybe the concept of saying something or doing something to bring about harmony, or doing harmony-chants or mantras, would be alright. I am very comfortable with just giving thanks and asking all things to come in harmony with the universe. Here is my prayer:

> May we always keep our feet on Mother Earth, our eyes and minds above the treetops, and our spirit with the Universal Spirit, as we walk the path of Good Medicine. Wah Doh.

This is the Spiritual Medicine Path. Good Medicine is not a replacement for, but a "way" to live along with a person's spiritual beliefs and spirit self.

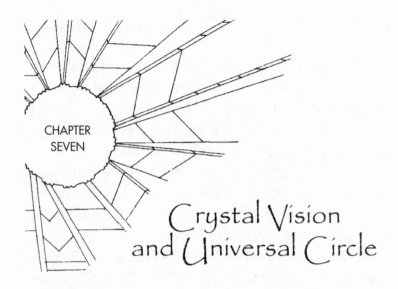

# Crystal Vision and Universal Circle

While walking in the Great Smoky Mountains near the Cherokee Reservation, I was looking for a special quartz crystal that would be waiting for me, as instructed by a Medicine Elder. She asked me to find my Crystal Vision by finding my special crystal. I was somewhat confused about how finding a crystal would focus my vision. She said, "The Crystal Vision is being able to see and feel your spiritual purpose. The crystal is more than just an energy stone. It is a spirit being with the healing energy of the Sun. It merges with our energy, or it may 'feel' hot or repel like a magnet. Once merged or having the connection with our energy, there is a special feeling or awareness. You feel a spirit movement or a tingle that you know is powerful. Learning how to use the crystal is healing in itself, as you begin to go on a path of a Crystal Vision. It is not a process as much as an experience." Understanding this took me about four years, as bits and pieces of visions or experiences came to me.

It is important to understand that the human being in the Universal Circle is not of greater power or purpose than anything else. Earlier stories tell Native Americans that the energy of the Great One is in everything that exists in the universe; therefore, we must demonstrate respect for everything, every moment of every day. This requires "spirit awareness" of all life, and that includes the rocks and minerals. This spirit awareness is enhanced by meditation, and by sensing the energy of plants and special rocks or crystals that acts to increase our spirit energy. As an Elder said, "It takes no special training to do this, just be a child." A crystal provides a sense of calm and balance, which is protection in itself. The Sacred Crystal was used by the early Cherokee spiritual leaders, just as the Sacred Pipe is used today by many tribes. Learning to use the quartz crystal also provides a balance and protection to our spirit self. It helps us to maintain control of the Four Directions.

"The light shining through a crystal is the Sun rising in the East and the Moon setting in the West, and is sacred," said the Elder. "Such light had a powerful message. In earlier times, a divining crystal was used by the spiritual clan leader, who would gather the families together in a room and wait until the Sun would rise in the East and pass through the crystal. While he or she would not touch the crystal, it was placed in such a way that the reflected light would pass over the people to clear them for the next Moon, or month. The Cherokee name for the crystal was based on the light shining through it, and only those initiated as spiritual leaders could keep the crystals used for these special purposes." The crystal was to remind us of a true and natural power that was protected by the "Little People" or the spirit people. Therefore,

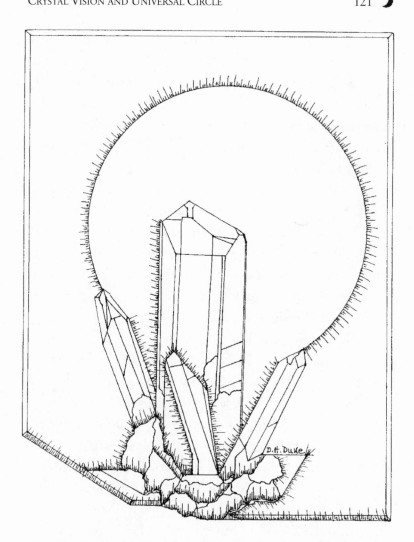

the crystal was highly respected as an honor stone. I was to learn about how to clear and use the crystal for Good Medicine from a particular Medicine Elder that has since passed on to the other world. She first told me to learn everything I could about the quartz crystal "from the book learning, then the right way." The quartz crystal is a mineral of silicone and oxygen produced by Mother Earth under

great pressure. The Cherokee understood the crystal to be
the spirit of a person who passed on and who was cleared by
Mother Earth or by a star person who is here to help balance
us. The physical compound of the crystal is silicone dioxide
with many varieties such as rock crystal, rose quartz, smoky
quartz, agate onyx, amethyst, bloodstone, jasper, and other
classifications of crystal. The hardness of the stone is recognized as about seven, reminding us of the Sacred Seven used
in Cherokee stories. (The turquoise of many western Native
Americans is held in respect the same way the Cherokee
honor the crystal. The Egyptians used the turquoise in similar ways during the First Dynasty in 5300 B.C.)

Quartz crystals are used in modern technology such as
detectors, CB radios, watches, and other devices used to
control frequencies. The Motorola Corporation uses a
hydrothermal process in Carlisle, Pennsylvania, to "grow"
quartz crystals for use in electronic devices. The natural
process of crystalline fusion of two common elements to
form silicone dioxide is a process of atoms bonding
together. Under tremendous pressure, these atoms arrange
in orderly and infinitely repeated three-dimensional patterns
called lattices. This makes the quartz harder than steel. The
irony is that people coming together with the same bonding
can create a will that is harder than steel, in a sense. Many
people today have crystals, but do not understand their
sacred value to Native Americans. The bonding that occurs
when energies merge between the energy of the crystal and
the person is like special friends coming together.

There has been some interesting work done on the
vibrations of crystals and the effect on the body's energy
field, using lines of energy similar to Chinese medicine with

acupuncture. As has been found in some biomagnetic research going on currently, the crystals produce a subtle energy that influences bio-organisms. These ideas came partly from work done around 1880 by two European scientists, Jacques and Pierre Curie, who subjected quartz to mechanical stress to generate electrical charges. The asymmetry of the crystal lattice makes crystals useful in electronics. The Curies found charges on the crystal surface by alternating electrical fields that cause rhythmic displacement of ions, known as "the piezoelectric effect." This technique is now used in instruments to sense earthquake activity, and is also very popular in electronic equipment. I have been told that a crystal oscillator set at 32,768 cycles per second is used in watches because it is stable at this frequency. Any slower or faster, and the watch is not accurate. Native Americans certainly have not gotten credit for the special knowlege and understanding of crystal energies. In my opinion, our ancestors were the first to "research" crystals for many uses, including protection, balancing, and healing. Certainly, they used them in healing and ceremonies.

The origin of the use of quartz crystals was based on a story about the Little People, who are the spirit people placed here to guide and teach us. As an Elder put it, "There was a simple answer for everything in earlier days. Now everything is more complex. We need to find simple answers again, to better deal with this complicated life. We can enjoy a special stone such as the crystal as being a gift from the Little People that has been cleared by Mother Earth to give us a little piece of a star." The crystal has its own special energy that the Cherokee say is connected to the Star Spirits. It is alright to accept or challenge that concept. However, test it for yourself. As the Elder said, "Listen real close on a moonlit night in the mountains or at the seashore. You can hear the Little People singing their prayer chants and dancing in the circle. If you don't hear it, it's OK, 'cause it is not your time to listen."

There are four sizes of quartz crystals, and one very sacred that is not to be shared or discussed. According to Cherokee traditions, two sizes of larger crystals were used only by war and peace chiefs, and one size only by a Medicine Man or Woman who was specially trained. A small crystal, about one-fourth to one inch in diameter, is used as a power crystal and kept near you in a room or in a purse or bag. Crystals smaller than one-fourth inch in diameter are to be worn around the neck, but in earlier years they would not be in sight. This size crystal can also be kept in a small Medicine Bag with some sacred tobacco or sage, and hung around the neck. One caution is to not wear it near the heart; let it hang just below the neck, or in a Medicine Bag on the belt or just kept in a pants pocket. If you want it for calming, then keep it in the left pants pocket or pointed in the direction of the North or the South. If you want it as a power crystal, keep it in the right pocket or pointed in the direction of the East or the West.

Are you wondering how to identify a power crystal or a calming crystal? In earlier times, one could just go to the Medicine Man or Woman and ask for a crystal to be "trained" a certain way. My best advice is to go to a rock shop, or any store where gemstones are sold, and find one that feels calm or comfortable to you. Ask your spirit self if this particular crystal would like to come home with you. Of course, you have to be careful that someone else is not around—just in case this person might think you have lost it, or the crystal might be talking to this other person. Hold it in your left hand between your thumb and forefingers as you sense how it feels to you. Also use your other senses, such as your vision, while holding it at arm's length; then slowly bring the crystal to within about seven inches of your breast to see how it *feels* to you. It is certainly alright to seek a crystal for yourself, or to be "gifted" with one from a special friend. Do remember that price is not a measure of Good Medicine when trying to find one. Your individual taste in style and clarity of crystals is your own choice.

..........................................................

## CRYSTAL HEALING

Crystals were used in earlier generations by many cultures. I was told that the native people of Brazil and Australia used crystals. In an art display I also saw a chieftain's wooden staff that came from the Taino natives who welcomed Columbus to the Caribbean; the wooden cane or staff contained a crystal that was very similar to the Cherokee crystals. I tried searching for clues as to its origin, but only found that up to 300,000 Taino lived in Jamaica and were predominant in the western Caribbean when Europeans arrived. These people grew corn and dug sweet potatoes, and they were potters and weavers in a culture that vanished in about the sixteenth century. I also found where five concentric stone circles were located in the Middle East, based on a culture of people that flourished about 5000 years ago. I was told by a Natchez-Cherokee Elder that a location with five circles would be discovered to have crystals in certain patterns to represent the Four Directions. These circles had a northeast gate that lined up with the summer solstice sunrise. Similar groupings were used by the early Cherokee with a sacred quartz crystal in each circle for certain sacred ceremonies. One of these ceremonies was the Sun Dance, with a pole in the middle and four poles that represented the Four Directions just inside the last circle. Certainly, there is still much to learn about how other cultures all over the world used crystals for adornment, healing, and ceremonies.

When we use the expression that something is "crystal clear," there is probably a Cherokee somewhere saying that we have finally learned to "read" the crystal and understand its spiritual power in clearing our lives. The Cherokee and other Native American tribes had secrets protected by the keepers on how to seek the crystal vision for healing. Instead of thinking "New Age," think "Old Wisdom" when it comes to crystals. I was reluctant to share some of this information during the past few years when the crystal fad was so popular. Now it is time to share some of these earlier teachings during the coming years of imbalance and unrest within and on Mother Earth.

The use of the quartz crystal by the early Cherokee has significant meaning for us today. As an Elder said, "Most people would walk by this little crystal and just look at it. Some might even just stick it in their pocket or pick it up and chunk it aside. I see the little crystal and say, 'How are you little crystal. You are so pretty. Would you like to work with me for awhile?' Some would probably say, 'Look at that old fool, talking to a rock!' Well, who is really the fool? The crystal lets you know if it is alright to pick it up; then, by feeling the energy, you can see if it is comfortable with you. If not, you put it back in the ground." Like us, the crystal needs to be "grounded" to Mother Earth.

The quartz crystal was considered to be a little spirit with energy as a helper to us. As an Elder said, "We need all the help we can get, especially in learning how to respect Nature and the gifts provided for us to protect and enjoy." When the crystal gets cloudy or tainted by negative energies and pollution, it is returned to the Earth Mother for "clearing." It is possible to clear crystals in unpolluted water, such as sea water or from a clear mountain spring, for a period of at least seven days. The point is that "clearing" was necessary for these little spirits to heal and to be helpers for us to heal. Could it be possible that many of our illnesses and conditions could be resolved by a "clearing?" Once I asked a Medicine Elder who said, "The problem with human beings is that they have choices and memory. The crystal has memory, too, but it is without influences, except when misused or subjected to negative energy again. Human beings think too much! It is the thinking and the attitude that gets in the way. They must learn to just accept more and be closer to Nature to heal."

..................................................

## HEALING ENERGY

Everything in Nature has energy, including the Sun, wind, and water. The Sun emits radiant energy and provides light, which includes ultraviolet and infrared heat radiation. The heating of Earth causes winds, and the evaporation of water forms clouds. This is the same energy used by plants and trees to convert carbon dioxide into water and food through the process of photosynthesis. We use the oxygen produced by the plants to live. Of course, Mother Earth stores other energy of living organisms that have been con-

verted into coal and oil. The energy in Nature is in harmony
with everything else in the environment. While in recent
years there has been a concern with exposure to ultraviolet
light, the Cherokee Elders say that Sun is as important as
other essential nutrients for life. We are now beginning to
better understand the optimal range of dosage of light for
peak health and biological functioning. I learned through the
Cherokee stories and through experience that almost everyone needs exposure to the full spectrum of the Sun's light. It
has to do with the natural energy interaction and balancing.
We do know that each kind of microorganism has a specific
frequency of interaction with the electromagnetic spectrum.
As the Natchez-Cherokee Elder said, "Light from the Sun is
both male and female, as energy, and it keeps us balanced
and in resonance with our own inner-spirit as we walk or just
relax in the sunshine. Of course, we should not be overex-
posed, but we need the warm energy of the Sun."

As we are the keepers of the Earth Mother, it is our
responsibility to protect and restore her harmony and balance whenever we take anything from her. When we receive
the gift of a crystal or anything special, we are to remind ourselves that we are now the protector of the gift, until we gift
someone else. It also reminds us of the energy we cannot see
that is part of the "spirit work" all around us: Each thing in
Nature having a purpose and we being the keepers and protectors for this wonderful world around us. As an Elder said,
"When you are the keeper, it is like you are the parent who
must nurture the Nature, as the Great One cares for us as an
energy or spirit being. The Crystal Vision reminds us of our
responsibility to be the special keeper and protector of
Mother Earth. We are to appreciate and respect her gifts of

energy stones of all kinds, the quartz crystal being just one.

We learned in school about potential energy that lies motionless and kinetic energy that is in motion. Science knows very little about "spirit" energy. It is there just like potential energy, just waiting to be put into motion to work for us. The transfer of energy is referred to as conduction, while convection is when heat moves from one place to another. In Indian Medicine, energy is to be used in natural motion for calming and healing. Energy is thought of as absorbed or directed to create either harmony or interference. As an example, the eagle feather or a crystal can be moved slowly across a person's body surface without touching it, to comb the energy fields to restore calm. The hands might be used to touch someone in a spot where there is energy blockage to stimulate or to calm the area or the person. It is also important to our harmony to have the energy of plants around us to promote healing. As an Elder said, "We can relearn these things, but always remember to ask permission before touching anything or anyone. We don't want to violate anything or anyone's space." Try asking permission before going into a wooded or park area, or before crossing a stream. See how it makes you feel or how it feels different to show respect and honor to Nature. Just holding a clear quartz crystal in your hand or laying it under your pillow can act to calm your energies and call forward good dreams for guidance.

There is much wisdom in the old teachings about using other energy for healing. As a "feel" test, sit near some plants that are within the reach of your arm or sit under a tree. Let yourself sense the feelings you get such as tingling, stimulation, calm, and particularly feel or sense the energy being given off by the plants or tree. As the Elder taught me, "With a little practice at doing nothing but being, you can learn to communicate with the plants and trees." If nothing else, you are allowing your body and mind to relax and heal itself. Try to notice anything that seems out of place, such as some trash lying on the ground. Does the environment seem in balance? How does someone else entering the picture change the energies? How about you, how do you feel in this place? Do you have a sense of being protected and feel relaxed?

While in the special place or "sacred spot" under the tree or with plants around you, hold a feather of a bird or a quartz crystal. Can you sense or feel the difference in holding the item as opposed to not holding it? If so, why do you think there is a difference? You can have some interesting feelings and images come to mind. As the Elder would say, "There is no right or wrong answer to questions such as these. Each person has their own experience, and they feel the difference, each in their own way. To enhance the sense or feel, we have to practice acceptance and open our 'spirit mind' to allow sensitivity to difference. The difference is that everything has varying levels of energy, even the rocks."

As radiation of energy is either transmitted, reflected, or absorbed, so is spirit energy. If the energy of another person seems negative, as we think of it, we can place an energy barrier to protect ourselves by visualizing light energy surrounding us. The exercises on energy are much easier to do and to teach in a circle of friends in a gathering or healing circle. My son and I enjoy having gatherings to share with others about Full Circle and the Four Directions in learning about energy and healing. As an Elder said, "Teach others to understand choices about healing. While they may not understand the traditions, help guide them to bridge the gap as your vision has guided you. It will bring about understanding among the kind of people that can make a difference. You were given the gift of the Medicine. Not to share it will mean that you are not following your Medicine Path." Even though water can be changed to ice or steam, it is still water. This Law of Conservation of Energy also fits Indian Medicine teachings. Spirit energy is a little more difficult to understand, but regardless of how it is used, it is still spirit energy. We also want to conserve spirit energy, because it is neither created or destroyed. The Great One has already created the energy for us to use. How we use it for the good of all things may determine how long we will have it to use.

Healing energy is a sense of calm that unblocks or harmonizes the vibrations or frequencies that are out of control. We were given the ancient teachings for preservation and sharing. I am willing to share in hopes of encouraging a better respect, appreciation, and understanding of our role as keepers of the secrets for those yet to come into this world. Everything we do and allow to happen affects everything else in the universe. A lesson here was that all things are connected within the Universal Circle. Native Americans are reminded of this every time there is a ceremony or a powwow that brings people together within the circle of family, clan, and tribe, the intertribal, and the Universal Circle. The power of healing in the circle can be utilized for balance of everyone in the circle, once there is harmony.

Miracles happen! Maybe more importantly, significant healing results occur as indicated in numerous studies where support systems for the ill are strong with love and emotional support. Early Cherokee "helpers" would use noncontact

ways to direct healing energy. They would warm their hands
over a sacred fire, then use circular motions about seven
inches from the physical body to stir or unblock the natural
energy. They would also hold the hands upward to the sky
and picture in their minds the person they were about to
heal, then send the energy for healing. Other techniques
included drumming; smudging with sacred tobacco, cedar,
or sage; and using song-chants. The "helpers" would also use
contact ways such as touch—especially gentle pressure on key
spots—to relieve pain and to enhance energy movement for
the body to heal itself naturally. It is a wonderful technique
with a very good feeling when there is a slight energy rush
during the therapy. There are two key points to remember:
(1) The helpers are not to use their own energy, except to
conserve and to protect themselves; and (2) visionary means
are used to determine how, where, and what to do as they
draw on the Universal Spirit for guidance. The person seeking healing guides the helper through his or her dreams;
visions; a journey through the Four Directions; and other
activities for participation and self-healing. The key is not to
take choices away but to have persons in control of themselves. The use of herbs and teas can be very effective for
relaxation and healing. Feathers, beads, and other traditional
Native American ceremonial tools are used in sacred ways.
This is the Energy Medicine, based on ancient ways or teachings held by the keepers of the secrets.

••••••••••••••••••••••••••••••••••••••••••••••••••••••••

## THE CRYSTAL VISION

The Crystal Vision comes when we are in harmony and balance with everything around us. The ancient ways taught us to focus on the level of harmony and balance in healing, rather than on the identity and condition of a disease and a possible modality of treatment. Seeing the "way" of renewing balance was more important than the individual problem or behavior being experienced. We experience outward expression of the ills of the family, clan, and tribe in the natural environment. Therefore, the family and the environment were included in the treatment. As a Medicine Elder once said, "The 'tree-ment' is to sit under a big oak tree long enough to work things out with the spirit helpers. They can give us a Crystal Vision to see what we cannot see for ourselves." He went on, "We are all brothers and sisters. We haven't learned a lot that is new, but just keep relearning the same lessons over and over again until we get it right." I was told over and over by the Native American Elders that the very best we can do in this life is to be a Good Medicine helper. That is what we finally come to in seeking our Crystal Vision.

The new medicine of tomorrow is here today. All we need to do is seek our "Crystal Vision" of what feels right and works for us. While advances will continue in modern medicine, the same old lessons will still be here. Being able to combine some of the old and new as "modern" rather than referring to it as "alternative and complementary" is the way of the future. The future must be focused on "Integrated Medicine and Health." Instead of being focused on our dietary or eating habits, supplemental plans for letting weight go and lowering blood fats could be based on energy activities and exercises of the future. These plans could include physical, mental, spiritual, and natural aspects based on *reversal* approaches rather than a *treatment* approach. Examples of such trends are the uses of antioxidants, distilled water, or exercises to reverse cellular damage and aging. Indian Medicine is a form of Integrated Medicine and Health in a culturally oriented segment of our population. It is based on energy balancing and harmony with everything in the Universal Circle, and can become a trend, not just an alternative, in all medicine and health.

The medicine of the future will focus on balance of the mind, body, and spirit using variations of activities such as yoga or t'ai chi as physical medicine. Surgery will be a replacement therapy based on physical balance and replacement where regenerative and gene therapies are not able to correct imbalance. The way we breathe and *what* we breathe are very critical to health and healing, and will be even more important in the future. Relaxation can be enhanced by combinations of very mild exercises. Those of us who do not care that much for sweat in exercise will really enjoy the new exercise of tomorrow. Use of simple healing and "helping" such as Reiki will be a healing exercise to strengthen and reverse destructive activity in the body of tomorrow. Massage therapies of the future will combine touch and attention to key points on the body that focus on release areas using energy "focalizers," so to speak. Reflexology will be extremely useful in combination with hydrotherapy and aromatherapy as practiced over 5000 years ago by the Egyptians, bringing about harmony among systems affecting the body/mind/spirit using the natural environment. The Energy will be used for ionizing, magnetizing, and energizing the air we breathe and the water we drink in the future. We will have tremendous capability to have distilled drinks that have been oxygenated with "energy enhancements" and supplements. As one Elder put it, "It will be heaven on Earth to have these treatments, in the future. I will just sit in the healing water and say, 'Give me one of those energy drinks so I can swim ten miles,' when I am ninety-two years old." Music with enhanced frequencies will be used to stimulate and relax in alternate and balancing ways. Of course, everything mentioned is already here, but not integrated fully with preventive medicine and health in our society for all people.

In the future, the nutritional and natural therapies will include minerals that will be combined for energy. Substances from life long ago will be rediscovered and will be used as new medicines. Biofeedback will become an exciting way to enhance transformation and energy emergence with the body and mind. Methods of "energy-checks" will be introduced for anyone to learn how to "focus" and get "readback," rather than just feedback. As an example, we will find out how to utilize the mind-body feedback systems, which are extremely accurate compared to mechanical feedback methods. We could be able to learn how to move to the spirit level for continuous feedback that would override the mind-body as "energy-checks" on such things as alcohol or sugar-level controls. The whole concept of visualization and imagery could be heightened to a level of CFSS or "Continuous Feedback Spirit Systems." The future could be an exciting time for increasing our ability to communicate within ourselves and with others on various energy levels. How are we to change the "could" to action that will get us to Integrated Medicine and Health? First, we must crystalize the vision of what we want, then seek it! In our society, as the expression goes, "Money talks!" When we are willing to pay or change regulations and requirements to provide what we want, guess what, we will get there. We have already started integrating these various therapies in a renewed Crystal Vision.

Support and teaching systems, or networks of inner-circles, are coming together to include every type of educational program and support group to be here at the touch of a fingertip. It will actually be done with imagery-electronics, allowing us to have video images right in our own homes. The approach will use the techniques of "Trans-Spirit-Communications" aided by light or "spiritronic" means. We will be able to dial in our support group and have them sitting in the same room with us, by having "Scottie, beam them up," so to speak. The teaching networks or inner-circles will be able to inform us, guide us, and help keep us on track in harmony and balance. This is an exciting future that is not anything like the pictures painted by some. This vision is real!

........................................................

### THE MEDICINE VISION

Once I asked an Elder to share his vision of the future Medicine. After much meditation, and as we threw some chicken feed to the chickens, the Medicine Elder said, "Look at what we have done to the chickens. Get some of that food in your hand. What happens? The chickens see you get the food out of the bag and they come begging. They are conditioned and we are conditioned. It is now time to uncondition ourselves and relearn some sacred and old ways of survival, choice, and honor for who we really are as the human spirits. It is time to put the warmakers in their place and the negative-thinkers into healing negativity. It is time for us as spiritual beings to become known as leaders of Good Medicine. It is time for us to heal ourselves and share as the Keepers of the Secrets. It is time to heal the Universal Circle." As the ancient ones taught us, we are the original people, meaning that we have all the memories of everything since the beginning of time. Learn to accept it and use it to benefit everyone and everything in the Universe.

Sometimes it is difficult for me to understand that the Medicine Vision may come in pieces, like short film strips. I also have to remind myself that guidance is there for the asking, but I also must be patient. A very close friend of mine had cancer. I could see the tumor, physically and how it had spread, in my mind's eye. He tried everything and spent a great deal of money on modern and alternative therapies, to no avail. I felt frustrated that I could not help him. I felt somewhat frustrated with therapies that did not work for him. He was full of life, and he loved everything and everybody. He lived the perfect healthy life! Why did he have to pass on, I kept asking myself over and over. In my last phone call from him, he said, "I know I have licked it! I will be clear in June." There was a pause, and he said, "Brother, I love you, and that is all that really matters. Will you do a tobacco prayer and clearing with me?" Gladly I accommodated him, and sadly I knew the truth. The truth of the Medicine Vision was that love is what really matters!

...............................................................

## THE PATH OF GOOD MEDICINE

My special friend lived the path of Good Medicine. The story of Indian Medicine is the story of choosing our path of healing for physical, mental, spiritual, and natural ways of life and life hereafter. The Native American Elders that I had the honor of studying with taught me about life from a very "grass-roots" perspective. One of the greatest lessons I learned was about humility and how it really is Medicine power. As an Elder said, "Humility is one lesson you *will* learn, even if you don't want to. You can learn it by honoring someone, or by learning it the hard way, but you're going to learn it. Why not learn about humility by honoring an Elder or helping someone who would truly appreciate you being a helper." After taking a trip on the mountain, experiencing grief, and coming to a calm point about my special friend, I realized that a "helper" was truly the best I could be.

The Four Directions provide a way or teaching about balance and the importance of finding harmony. As a member of the Eastern Band of Cherokee, my story of Indian Medicine has that perspective. However, there are many similar teachings in every culture of people around the world. Instead of focusing on the aspect of what was done wrong to us, Native American Elders say to take that as a lesson and come together as people of all races, colors, and beliefs in the Universal Circle. We were given the gift of thinking; therefore, we can decide, make choices, and even change our own attitudes at will. We can choose our own path to follow in the Four Directions, and we can change those directions at will. We can also find balance in our lives and choose the path of harmony, instead of disharmony, at will. And after all is said and done, there is no ending to the story of Indian Medicine, only another beginning.

· · · · · · · · · · · · · · · · · · · · · · · · · · · · · · · · · · · · · · · · · · · · · · · · ·

## THE UNIVERSAL CIRCLE

You have already started your Crystal Vision by reading this book. It has been enjoyable for me to share, but I know that many of the thoughts and words used require some thought on your part to merge some of this into your thinking and choices. To summarize the Four Directions we have gone through to get to our Crystal Vision, I offer the following guide to the Universal Circle:

**South:** Direction of the Natural
Path of Peace
color: white
Relearn to think, play, and love as a child. Get into a circle with friends, find a special rock, and play with a pet animal or bird. Plant a tree or flowers and touch Mother Earth.
*The key is innocence.*

**West:** Direction of the Physical
Path of Introspection
color: black
Enjoy some competition, learn to "dance" physically for confidence, and "be" intro-spective. Be a helper to someone, physically.
*The key is to help those less fortunate.*

**North:** Direction of the Mental
Path of Quiet
color: blue (or blue-white)

Learn something new, share some time on a
hike or trip to the mountains with a special
friend, and share your wisdom with others.
*The key is sharing and teaching.*

**East:**    Direction of the Spiritual
Path of the Sun
color: red
Come together with family and friends on a
spiritual journey. Gift others with a kind
thought or deed. Seek harmony and find a
place for prayer and ceremony.
*The key is coming together and honoring
the Elders.*

I sat alone on the rock where my Grandfather Rogers
and I sat many years before by the Oconaluftee River in the
Smoky Mountains. I could hear his voice carried in the wind
saying, "The Great One honors you with life, and you must
honor the Great One in life. You do that by honoring your
mother and father and all of life. One day you will come to
realize your spiritual gift. Gift others with the wisdom as you
'bridge the gap.' Know that the healing energy is in every
plant and tree, in every mineral from Mother Earth and in all
that she provides, and in the water of the river and in the
ocean. Understand that you are to teach healing as taught by
the ancestors of our people of the Red Clay. Seek guidance
from the spirit people. Remember that the secret is love in all
its many forms. Give thanks."

**Prayer:** Oh Great One, thank you for this day. Thank
you for all things in the Universal Circle. I will be a keeper of
the wisdom and a protector of Mother Earth. I will be a

helper. May my heart and spirit always be in harmony with the Universal Spirit. Guide me to know my vision as I walk the path of Good Medicine. Oh Great One, "Wah Doh" (thank you).

# PART TWO

## TO WALK IN BEAUTY:

# The Way of Right Relationship

by

Michael Tlanusta Garrett, Ph.D.
Eastern Band of Cherokee

# The Sacred Dance

At dawn, in the stillness of shadows, a young boy and a young girl, both adorned with eagle feathers, dance in celebration of the new day, honoring the sacredness of life and connection with all things in Creation. The little dancers step lightly on the moist soil, fresh with the dewdrops of an evening's sleep, blessed in the gentle light of Grandmother Moon and the little Star People. The dancers flap their little arms eagerly in the quiet awakening somewhere between Mother Earth and Father Sky, honoring the spirit of our brother, the eagle. They feel their hearts beating, and so, too, they feel the heartbeat of all creation pulsing through their veins, the pulsing spirit of their ancestors before them, of those to come, and that of all things in the Greater Circle.

As the little dancers breathe, Earth breathes slowly, evenly, surely. As they flow like the water of rivers and rainfall with its purifying and healing energies, the life energy of all things flows in constant motion, unbroken, undisrupted in its beauty. As they dance, the wind dances, carrying the sacred message of calm to each of the leaves in the trees, each of the little plant people, each of the rock people, and all of the animals. As the little ones smile the smile of ageless wonder with eyes wide, the Sun rises, bringing warmth and light to all living things.

The young boy and the young girl dance and are grateful with each step they take as a sacred offering, a giving of thanks for all our relations. All things in the Greater Circle of Life dance in harmony and balance, and it is good. And for all this, we have much to be thankful.

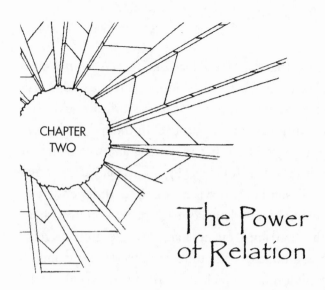

# The Power
## of Relation

I n the traditional Medicine Way, we call upon "all our relations" for strength, for guidance, for wisdom. We give
thanks to "all our relations," to the Great Creator, to each
of the Four Directions, to Father Sky, to Mother Earth, and
to all the elements. All of these things have life of their own,
and all of these things are sacred. Each one has a sacred reason for existing and a purpose to fulfill in the greater scheme
of things. All of these things are to be respected as a special
part of the Greater Circle of Life. And it is the "relation" of
each part to the others that creates a special flow in energy,
called "life."

By honoring "relations" in the way that we live each day,
in the way that we think, and act, and breathe, we are honoring that sacred flow of energy called "life." And it is through
this flow of energy, through all parts of the Greater Circle of
Life, that we not only survive, but really *live* and experience
life in its fullest beauty. This is the power of relation.

From the dawn of time, humankind has witnessed indi-

viduals banding together in the face of adversity for the sake
of survival. Mutual protection and support are the traditional
functions of relational bonds that have historically held people together with a common purpose. In the old days, individual survival rooted itself in the survival and well-being of
the group. This was true for all groups of peoples at one time
or another. Essentially, survival required independence
based on the interdependence of each person on the other.
Although the hardships facing many people are different
today, both in kind and magnitude, than those of our ancestors, one common fact remains: People need people. This,
too, is the power of relation. We need others to survive, and
we enjoy the presence of others to live.

Whether we realize it or not, whether we like it or not,
we live in a world where each part affects and is affected by
every other part. Contrary to what many individualists would
expect, we do not merely exist, we *co-exist*. We live in relation to everything else in this world—all of the plant people,
the tree people, the rock people, the bird people, the fish
people, our four-legged brothers and sisters of the animal
world, and all other living things.

In the many traditions of Indian Medicine, there is also
a strong, active, and reciprocal relationship between our
physical world and the "Above World" or spirit world. We are
connected not only with the spirit energy of every living thing
here in this physical world, but also with the spirit of our
ancestors and those to come. We are as leaves on a tree
whose roots extend deeply into the body and spirit of
Mother Earth, and from whom branches will continue to
stretch themselves toward the eternally blue silence of Father
Sky, giving life to new leaves whose beauty and presence

serve to strengthen and renew the essence of its roots.

There is an old story that, at one time, we humans were little spirits, who out of curiosity decided to come into physical form to experience life in a different way and to grow. Since then, as with all things, we have become part of the Greater Circle of Life in many aspects and forms. Thus "relationship," not only to other things, but to life itself and to ourselves, is constant and ever-flowing. And, in our lives, the presence and importance of "relationship" permeates every living moment, from the day that we are born until the day that we "cross over" into the other world.

In Cherokee tradition and beliefs, we move through four realms of being as we live and grow. The first realm occurs with birth and with the expanding realization that we are alive, "a presence of mind" symbolized by a child's first smile. The second realm is adolescence with our young person's exploration and development of special strengths, talents, and abilities that we uniquely have to offer. The third realm of being is marked by adulthood, where we have sufficiently developed the means for assisting family, clan, tribe, and community as we deepen the inner vision. The fourth realm occurs as we become an Elder or a "keeper of the wisdom" around age fifty-one or fifty-two, when we have developed the ability to offer methods of harmonization through understanding of relationships and the force of our own nature and energy.

The Elder, or "wise child," reveres the wisdom of the world and maintains a sense of mystery and wonder, never forgetting the importance of the first smile. Becoming an Elder is coming to a place of clarity through thought and action, and through being. This is true "presence of mind."

And this is possible through our recognition and "feeling" of where we stand in relation to everything else. Presence of mind occurs through an honoring of all relations, and through an understanding of our own "Medicine" and what we have to share. Everything has purpose in the Greater Circle.

Many tribes speak of the Circle of Life or the Web of Life, which is truly an appropriate description of the complex set of relationships in which we all live. Our world, whether intrapersonal, interpersonal, natural, or universal, is like a great big spider web in which each strand is dependent on every other strand for existence and for balance. Picture a spider web glistening in the morning light. That is our Circle of Life. As a matter of fact, the old Cherokee legend describing the First Fire centers around the sacredness of our little sister, the Water Spider.

In the beginning, a long, long time ago, there was no fire and the world was cold. So the Red Thunder Beings in the Above World sent their lightning and put a fire in the bottom of a hollow sycamore tree that grew on a small island. All the animals knew that the fire was there because they could see the smoke and they could feel a little bit of its warmth, even from that distance. They wanted to be close to the fire and warm themselves but couldn't because the old sycamore tree was on an island that they could not easily reach.

The animals held council in order to decide what must be done about the situation. All the animals were there including Raven, Screech Owl, Hooting Owl, Horned Owl, Racersnake, Blacksnake, and Water Spider. Needless to say, all of the animals who could fly or swim were eager to go after the fire. The first one to come forward was Raven, saying, "I will bring back the fire for all of us." And all the animals thought that Raven would be the best one since he was so big and strong. So Raven was first to go.

He flew high and far over the water to where the island was, and landed easily on the sycamore tree. But while he was wondering what to do, the heat scorched all his feathers black, and it frightened him so much, he came squawking back without the fire. To this day, Raven is black from being scorched by the heat.

The next one offering to go after the fire was little Screech Owl, saying, "I will bring back the fire for all of us." He flew high and far over the water and landed on the sycamore tree. But while he was looking down into the hollow tree, a blast of hot air came up and nearly burned out his eyes. He flew back as best he could . . . and without the fire. It was a long time before he could see well again. To this day, little Screech Owl's eyes are red.

Horned Owl and Hooting Owl were next to go after the fire, saying, "We will bring back the fire for all of us." They flew high and far over the water and landed on the sycamore tree. But by the time they got there, the fire was burning so fiercely that the smoke nearly blinded them, and the ashes carried up by the wind put white rings around their eyes. Horned Owl and Hooting Owl came back without the fire and no matter how much they rubbed their eyes, they couldn't get rid of the white rings. To this day, both Horned Owl and Hooting Owl have white rings around their eyes.

Now, none of the other birds would dare to go after the fire, seeing what had happened to Raven and the Owls. So the little Racersnake spoke up and said, "I will bring back the fire for all of us." Everyone thought he might have a good chance of doing just that because he was small and very quick.

Little Racersnake swam quickly across the water to the island and crawled through the grass to the sycamore tree, going into a small hole at the bottom. The heat and smoke were unbearable for the little Racersnake, who dodged blindly over the hot ashes until he was almost on fire. When he finally managed to get out again through the same hole, his whole body was scorched black. Ever since then, little Black Racersnake has a habit of darting and doubling back on his track as if trying to escape from the fire.

By now the animals were getting very worried because they still had no fire. Just then, a great big snake, the Climber, volunteered to go after the fire, saying, "I will bring back the fire for all of us." So off he went, swimming easily across the water to the island. When he got to the sycamore tree, he climbed up from the outside the way snakes like him always do. But when he put his head into the hole, the smoke choked him, and he fell into the burning stump. When he finally managed to get free, his whole body was as black as charcoal. He, too, returned without the fire, and to this day is called Blacksnake.

Several of the animals had bravely gone after the fire and come back without it. All of the animals were very worried because it was cold and still they had no fire, so they held another council. Now, all the other animals had thought up reasons why they couldn't go after the fire because, deep down, they were all afraid that if they went near the sycamore tree, they too would get burned. All the animals refused to go, except for one, and that was the little Water Spider. She had black downy hair and red stripes on her body. She could run on top of the water or dive to the bottom.

The little Water Spider listened patiently in council as the animals talked about their situation with great dismay, and when it came time for her to speak, she said quietly, "I will bring back the fire for all of us." All of the animals wondered how the little Water Spider could do that, and some even began to laugh at the very thought. After all, she wasn't very big, and she wasn't very strong. How could she bring back the fire?

"I'll find a way," said the Water Spider, and with that she began to weave a bowl from spun thread and then fastened it upon her back. She crossed the water and went through the grass where the fire was still burning. She put one small coal into her bowl and brought it back for all of the animals. Everyone rejoiced, and the animals built a sacred fire from the coal, around which they all danced in celebration for many days. Since that time, we have had fire, and to this day, the little Water Spider still keeps her bowl. And so, it is good.

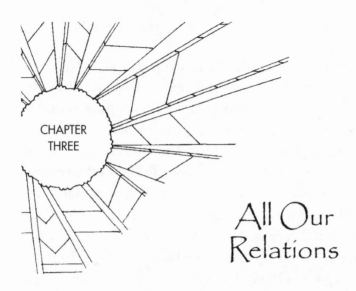

# All Our
# Relations

I t has been said by Wynne Hanson DuBray, a Rosebud
Sioux, that "about the most unfavorable moral judgment
an Indian can pass on another person is to say, ' He acts
as if he didn't have any relatives'." The concept of "relation"
is a way of life for many Native American people and it is very
important, for good reason. Everything is thought of in terms
of relation of one kind or another. That is the natural order
of things. It is thus believed that we cannot possibly know
where we stand without knowing where we are in relation to
everything else. Upon meeting for the first time, many Native
American people will ask, "Where do you come from, who's
your family?" This is because they are wanting to know where
they stand in relation to this new person, and what commonality exists. In fact, this is a simple way of building
bridges ... or recognizing bridges that already exist but are as
yet unknown. It is also a way of honoring those bridges by
appreciating them for what they are, and by sharing.

We are connected with all things, and we need only discover this truth to discover the power and beauty of relation. In the traditional way, we call upon all our relations for strength, guidance, and wisdom. We call upon our relations for comfort and for sharing. There is harmony and balance in the energy of our connections. And it is believed that one of the most powerful sources of strength and wisdom comes from the family with whom we are truly connected. Of course, family may or may not consist of blood relatives. It is common practice in the Native American traditional way, for instance, to "claim" another as a relative, thereby welcoming him or her as real family. From that point on, that person *is* a relative and that is that. After all, "family" is a matter of blood, *and* of spirit.

"Family" may be certain friends that have stuck by us through the years. It may be the parents who have sacrificed for us, protected us, and stuck by us through thick and thin. It may be an Elder who has guided us through rough times and through good ones. It may be a special teacher who has always believed in us. It may be a pet that always seems to be there when we need him or her. It may even be a virtual stranger whom we met only recently, but somehow "really hit it off with" from the first, with or without realizing that there is a special connection. You see, one universal truth that guides the whole of our experiences is that the spirit does not keep time; it only records growth. We need not have known someone for a long, long time to *really* know them, or to feel a special connection with them. And this is an important opportunity for learning and for sharing. These are the things the spirit holds most dear.

Think of all the special people in your life now, and all the special people that have been in your life during your time on Mother Earth. There's a very special feeling as the faces come to mind. Take a little time to see them all. Maybe certain experiences come to you—something funny that happened, for example, or a difficult time that was shared with another, and endured. What you feel is the energy of these connections that is a part of your essence and your memories. This is the blood of your spirit running warmly through you. It is from the energy of these connections that we draw much strength and guidance. It is also through these powerful connections that we receive much wisdom, understanding, and growth—even if we have to get it the hard way. There is an old Cherokee story about the origin of strawberries that relates this lesson very well.

A long, long time ago, when Mother Earth was young, the Great One created a man and a woman who lived together in harmony and loved each other very much. Things were going very well for the man and woman until one morning when the woman became very angry with the man and walked out of their lodge, slamming the door shut behind her.

The man, who did not understand why the woman had become so angry, thought to himself, "She must not be feeling well," and left it at that. Hours passed, and the woman did not return. The man began to worry and went outside to look for her, but she was gone. Way off in the distance, he could see her climbing the mountain to the west, and he began to get little tears in his eyes. He set off after her, but he knew that she was too far away, and he would not be able to catch up. Now he was crying out of sadness for losing her, and he began to pray with his head in his hands.

"O Great One," he pleaded desperately, "I love her so very much, and she has gone away. I will never be able to catch up, and I do not know what to do."

"What is the problem?" asked the Great One. This made the man a little angry because the Great One is supposed to know everything that happens and why. Besides that, the man didn't really know what the problem was, or why the woman had left. He was very sad though, and could not think straight, but he did his best to explain what he knew.

"Are you sure you did not do anything?" asked the Great One.

"I don't know," replied the man.

"Are you sure that you did not fail to do something?" asked the Great One.

"I'm not sure," sighed the man. "She is getting further and further away, and I do not know what to do."

"I know that your love for her is great, and your heart is true," said the Great One. "I will do what I can to slow her down."

The man expressed much thanks, and continued on his journey up the mountain.

Meanwhile, the Great One caused a huckleberry bush full of ripe huckleberries to spring up along the woman's path. But the woman was so angry that she ignored the huckleberries, and didn't even slow down.

Next, the Great One put some prickly blackberries along her path, thinking that the blackberries would stick to her clothes and make her slow down. As the woman walked through the blackberries, they stuck to her clothes, but she just ignored them, and didn't even look down.

"Aha!" thought the Great One. "I must make her look down in humility before she will stop and listen to what is in her heart." So he put a little plant on the ground with leaves that hid a luscious, sweet-smelling fruit shaped like a heart.

When the woman came to the little plant, the aroma was so wonderful that she got down on her knees to find out what smelled so good. When she bowed her head to pick one of the fruits and saw the beautiful little heart-shaped berries, she let go of her anger, and forgot why she had been angry in the first place.

The first thing she thought was to pick some of these delicious strawberries for her husband, whom she loved with all her heart. She picked only the smaller ones so that the big ones could grow, and she gave thanks to Mother Earth and the Great One for offering this special gift. Then she started back home, toward the east.

Before long, she saw her husband in the distance coming toward her. Excitedly, she ran to him, and they hugged each other for a very long time in the setting Sun. Then she gave him the bright red strawberries she had picked for him, and together they gave thanks to the Great One for being reunited once again.

The woman thought about how sad she would have been to never see her husband again. She told him that she would never leave him, and just then, she noticed that the little strawberries were very fragile, and yet very beautiful. The man and the woman were thankful for their love of one another, and together they enjoyed the sweet, juicy strawberries that the Great One had provided to Mother Earth. And so, it is good.

Our connections serve a very important purpose for us, just as we serve a very important purpose in the beauty of the Greater Circle. All things are connected, and we are all related. For this and more, we have much to be thankful.

The whole idea of "relation" is a very simple one, and yet, it is very powerful in the way that it guides a life, a way of thinking, a way of acting and being. Here, too, the idea of "being" is rooted in the notion that we need only seek our place in the universe; everything else will follow. But in order to do so, we must first honor all our relations, treating them with kindness and respect. We must see ourselves as a part of them, and them as part of us, and we must be thankful. All things are connected.

Let me illustrate, using an example given to me by Medicine Grizzlybear Lake, a Seneca/Cherokee. If we are walking in the woods together, and I bend down to pick up a stick, asking you, "What is this?" you might reply, "It is a stick." And what if I say, "No, it is part of a tree."?

When we humans were once little spirits and wanted to come into physical form, there was one condition placed upon us. The Great One, or Creator of All Things, allowed us little spirits to come into physical form knowing that when this happened, our awareness would be limited. This is the way of things, and it is the way in which we grow and move beyond ourselves. Perspective offers us powerful lessons, as with the strawberries, and with the little stick lying in the woods.

The lesson of the stick: We must see ourselves as part of the Greater Circle, no greater, no less, but part. All things are indeed connected, as Chief Seattle once affirmed, and we must honor all our relations by honoring and understanding the Universal Circle for what it is—a unity of interrelated and interdependent strands. The Web is not a web without each and every one of its strands serving its purpose, no matter how great or small.

All of this may sound complicated, but it is not. Things really only get complicated when we refuse to recognize the power of the whole, robbing ourselves and our world by see-ing only separate and unrelated parts, such as "unused resources," or "inanimate objects." It becomes even more complicated when we approach other people with the same mindset. This is a disruption in the natural flow of life energy and it is harmful to ourselves and to all other living things. Mother Earth is teaching us a hard lesson right now by react-ing to all our pollution, disrespect, and misuse of the gifts she has offered to us.

Still, she continues to offer all her gifts to us, asking only in return that we treat her with the kindness and respect that we expect from her, and from others. When the animals hold council, everyone's voice is heard and everyone is respected for their unique contribution to the Circle, even the little Water Spider. But everyone must give respect and kindness as well as receive it. Everyone must look for the beauty in all things, no matter how great or small. We must not only call upon all our relations for strength, guidance, and wisdom, but must be called upon in turn.

There is a traditional saying, "If you know my family, then you know me." We all must realize that, although we may come from different "tribes," we are all of the same fam-ily, and of one Mother.

# The "True" Meaning of Family

A long, long time ago, before Mother Earth existed as we know her today, there was only a planet of water surrounded by the universe. In Galun'lati, or "Sky World," the animals, plants, and rocks were very crowded and needed more room. What they all needed was a home. So all the animals, plants, and rocks held a great council in the Sky World to decide what must be done. Everyone's voice was heard in the great council, which lasted for many days, and when everything was through, it had been decided that the little Water Beetle would go down from the Sky World and dive beneath the water of the planet to see what he could find.

Little Water Beetle left the Sky World and dove beneath the shimmering blue water, going deeper and deeper. But he did not find a firm place until he reached the bottom. Then, with as much soft mud from the bottom of the great water as he could carry, Water Beetle swam back up to the surface. There, the mud spread and spread until it became the island, Earth.

In the beginning, Earth was wet and soft, so the council in the Sky World sent Great Buzzard out to search for a place where all living things could go. Great Buzzard flew down from the Sky World and soared over the soft Earth until he became very tired. Where his great big wings struck the Earth, there were valleys; and where he rose to the sky, there were mountains. This later became known as Cherokee country.

Now, all the animals, plants, and rocks, and even the little spirits, had a place where they could live, but there was still one problem. Earth was still very soft and wet. Next, the council in the Sky World asked for the help of Grandfather Sun, who agreed to do what he could. And so, the Sun moved slowly around Earth from east to west, giving light and warmth to the land. He was so impressed with its beauty that he, too, wanted to live in this new place, but he knew that he could not get too close because he was so hot and so bright that he would burn it up. So he decided to stay in the Sky World, but to always move around Earth, admiring her beauty, giving her light and warmth, and protecting her.

The animals, plants, and rocks in the Sky World were very excited about their new home; they thanked Grandfather Sun and agreed to greet him each morning when he rose in the east and give thanks. Soon, all the animals, plants, and rocks came down from the Sky World to live on Mother Earth, and some of the little spirits even came; these were the first people. And all lived together in harmony and balance as one family of many things, and all were thankful each day for life and for their beautiful Mother

Earth. This is the Cherokee story of how the world was made. And so, it is good.

We have always been of one family, and it is good to have life. In a single lifetime, we are given many gifts, not the least of which is Earth under our feet and the breath of life in our chest. And we all exist in "community" of one kind or another.

Because the survival and well-being of the individual is synonymous with that of the community, family plays a prominent role in our lives, whether we realize it or not. Many Native American people *are* a "family" in a real sense, because they identify themselves not by their own accomplishments, but by the nature of their relations and the energy they draw from those connections. However, it is important to realize that what the mainstream defines as "family" takes on a much broader view in the traditional way. Family relationships include much more than the biological connections of the nuclear family. For example, as mentioned before, the claiming of non-blood relatives as family members is commonly practiced among Native American people who try to listen to the "spirit" of the relationship and honor it accordingly. Very often, we come into this world with many relatives, not limited only to blood relations.

In the traditional way, the prevalence of cooperation and sharing in the spirit of community is essential for harmony and balance. It is not unusual for a Native American child to be raised in several different households over time— not because no one cares enough to keep him or her around very long, or because Native American people are lazy and irresponsible, but because it is considered both an obligation and a pleasure to share in raising and caring for the children in the family. Grandparents, aunts, uncles, and other members of the community are all responsible for the raising of children, and they take this responsibility very seriously. After all, children are the fresh green leaves unfolding on the outermost branches of the tree, and they give the tree and its roots much strength and beauty.

The traditional view of family is universal in scope. "Family" extends well beyond immediate relatives to extended family relatives through the second cousin, members of the clan, members of the community or tribe, all other living creatures in this world, the natural environment, and the universe itself. The entire universe is thought of as "a family" with each and every one of its members having a useful and necessary place in the Circle of Life, just as each strand creates the beauty and strength of the Web.

The animals are our four-legged brothers and sisters; Earth is our Mother; the Sky World, our Father; the Moon, our Grandmother; and the Sun, our Grandfather to all living creatures. All these are our relatives, and should be treated with kindness and respect deserved by any family member. Traditionalists believe that the connection we all have with others (not just people) is to be considered nothing short of sacred. "Relation" is something that extends beyond biological connection to one also of a spiritual nature. For every connection that we have, we are part of it and it is part of us. And there is energy in that, which we call "life." The traditional view of "family" symbolizes a unique approach to the entire process of living as we move through the Circle of Life.

In 1855, upon surrendering tribal lands to the governor of the Washington Territory, Chief Seattle of the Suquamish and Duwamish people delivered his famous speech with great eloquence and sadness. Following are adapted excerpts from words spoken by Chief Seattle:

Every part of this Earth is sacred to our people. Every shining pine needle, every sandy shore, every mist in the dark woods, every clearing, and every humming insect is holy in the memory and experience of our people. The sap which courses through the trees carries the memories of the people.

The perfumed flowers are our sisters; the Deer, the Horse, the great Eagle, these are our brothers. The rocky crests, the juices of the meadows, the body heat of the pony and people—all belong to the same family.

The ashes of our fathers and mothers are sacred. Their graves are holy ground, and so these hills, these trees, this portion of Earth is consecrated by us. The shining water that moves in the streams and rivers is not just water, but the blood of our ancestors. You must teach your children that it is sacred and that each ghostly reflection in the clear water of the lakes tells of events and memories in the life of our people. The water's murmur is the voice of our father's father.

The rivers are our brothers, they quench our thirst. The rivers carry our canoes and feed our children. You must teach your children that the rivers are our brothers, and you must give the rivers the kindness you would give any brother.

The air is precious to us, and it shares its spirit with all the life it supports. The wind that gave our grandfather and grandmother their first breath also receives their last sigh. And the wind must also give our children the spirit of life. When we taste the wind that is sweetened by the meadow's flowers, we must remember that it is sacred.

The animals are our brothers and sisters. What are we without the animals? If all the animals were gone, we would die from a great loneliness of spirit. Whatever happens to the animals, soon happens to the people. All things are connected.

You must teach your children that the ground beneath their feet is the ashes of our grandfathers and grandmothers. So that they will respect the land, tell your children that Earth is rich with the lives of our kin. Teach your children what we have taught our children, that Earth is our Mother. Whatever befalls Earth, befalls the sons and daughters of Earth.

This we know. Earth does not belong to people; people belong to Earth. This we know. All things are connected like the blood which unites one family. All things are connected.

Love the land as we have loved it. Care for it as we have cared for it. And with all your strength, with all your mind, with all your heart, preserve it for your children and love it . . . as the Great One loves us all.

# Harmony, Balance, and the Natural Flow

E verything around us is alive with spiritual energy and importance. This includes all animals, plants, people, rocks, and minerals; Earth, sky, Sun, Moon, and stars; and the elements, such as wind, water, fire, thunder, clouds, lightning, and rain—all combined in an intricate system of interdependence and interrelationship.

A fundamental belief in the Medicine Way is this: *All things are connected.* The universe is made up of a balance among all of these things and a continuous flow or cycling of this energy. We have a sacred relationship with the universe that is to be honored every moment of every day, through our thoughts, intentions, and actions. All things are connected, all things have life, and all things are worthy of respect and reverence.

# THE MEDICINE WHEEL

The Circle is a sacred symbol that reminds us that the entire universe moves and works in circles. At the very heart of the tradititional way of life is a worldview that emphasizes this Circle of Life represented by the Medicine Wheel. Its components—spirit, natural environment, body, and mind— symbolize the four sacred points on a circle or the Four Directions—East, South, West, and North—represented in this Circle of Life.

The Circle of Life symbolizes the innumerable circles that surround us, that exist within us, and of which we are all a part. It shows us the sacred relationship we have to all living things, to life itself. The Medicine Wheel thus serves as a reminder to honor the four sacred aspects of life and to seek harmony and balance in our own "way."

In the traditional way, "Medicine" refers to "the way of things," a way of life, or the essence of a living being. We each have our own "Medicine" or way of life through an essence and personal power wherein we choose which of the Four Directions to focus most of our energy, and how to seek our own harmony and balance. The Medicine Wheel symbolizes the way of things as represented in the Four Directions, each of which stands for one aspect of life:

East for **Spirit**
South for **Natural Environment**
West for **Body**
North for **Mind**

In seeking our "Medicine," we are seeking harmony and balance among these four directions, between ourselves and the universe. Being in harmony means being "in step with the universe" and with its sacred rhythms; likewise, being in disharmony means being "out of step with the universe." Therefore, it is always important for us to remember where we are in relation to everything else, and where we are in relation to ourselves. Carol Locust, a Cherokee, describes Native

American beliefs concerning illness:

> Each individual chooses to make himself well or to make himself unwell. If one stays in harmony, keeps all the tribal laws and all the sacred laws, one's spirit will be so strong that negativity will be unable to affect it. If one chooses to let anger or jealousy or self-pity control him, he has created disharmony for himself. Being in control of one's emotional responses is necessary if one is to remain in harmony. Once harmony is broken, however, the spiritual self is weakened and one becomes vulnerable to physical illness, mental and/or emotional upsets, and the disharmony projected by others.

Keeping in step with the universe means abiding by the natural laws of Creation. Violating these guiding principles means bringing discord, dissonance, and disharmony upon ourselves and others. A way of keeping in step with the universe is by listening, practicing patience, asking permission, and giving thanks. A way of seeking harmony within ourselves is to ask ourselves the following questions as posed by the medicine wheel, and to balance ourselves with the answers in whatever way is most comfortable to us:

East: **"Who or what am I a part of?"**
South: **"What do I enjoy doing or do well?"**
West: **"What are my strengths; what limits me?"**
North: **"What do I have to share or contribute?"**

The Medicine Way is a seeking of harmony within ourselves, with others, and with our surroundings through harmony and balance of personal, social, and environmental relationships. It emphasizes an active relationship between the physical and spirit worlds and the necessity of seeking harmony and balance with both. Careful attention is given to the Law of Reciprocity in which something is offered for everything that is respectfully taken in order to honor and maintain the harmony and balance of interrelationship and interdependence. Permission is asked whenever possible and thanks is given. This requires time and patience. It requires that we listen to what is in our hearts and to what is around us. Just as it never hurts to show appreciation for others by saying, "Thank you," it never hurts to show appreciation for all living things, for Mother Earth, and for life itself by simply saying, "Thank you."

Such views and practices emphasize what is considered the Sacred Way, and form the foundation for Native American spirituality and an honoring of "all our relations." Kindness, respect, generosity, and patience are not simply ways of acting, but ways of living and feeling. The way of harmony and balance is not a part of life, it *is* life. And when we live in accordance with the natural way of harmony and balance, we become part of the sacred flow in an ever-moving stream of life energy and natural beauty.

# The Way of
the Circle

The Medicine Way is based on an unwritten "code of ethics" that honors the natural laws of Creation to guide our way of life toward harmony and balance with all our relations—personal, social, and environmental. The "Way of the Circle" is passed down from generation to generation, from Native American Elders to the children in the form of stories, traditions, customs, and teachings. What follows is a general collection of these teachings, which can be embraced by anyone seeking the way of harmony and balance:

1. When you first arise in the morning, give thanks to the Creator (Great Spirit), to the Four Directions, to Mother Earth, to Father Sky, and to all of our relations, for the life within you, and for all life around you.

2. Remember that all things are connected.
    • All things have purpose, everything has its place.
    • Honor others by treating them with kindness and

consideration; always assume that a guest is tired, cold, and hungry, making sure to provide him or her with the best of what you have to offer.

3. If you have more than you need for yourself and your family, consider performing a "giveaway" by distributing your possessions to others who are in need.

4. You are bound by your word, which cannot be broken except by permission of the other party.

5. Seek harmony and balance in all things.

• It is always important to remember where you are in relation to everything else, and to contribute to the Circle in whatever way you can by being a "helper" and a protector of life.

• Sharing is the best part of receiving.

• Practice silence and patience in all things as a reflection of self-control, endurance, dignity, reverence, and inner calm.

• Practice modesty in all things; avoid boasting and loud behavior that attracts attention to yourself.

• Know the things that contribute to your well-being, and those things that lead to your destruction.

6. Always ask permission, and give something for everything that is received, including giving thanks for, and honoring, all living things.

7. Be aware of what is around you, what is inside of you, and always show respect.

• Treat every person from the tiniest child to the oldest Elder with respect.

• Do not stare at others; drop your eyes as a sign of respect, especially in the presence of Elders, teachers, or other honored persons.

• Always give a sign of greeting when passing a friend or stranger.

• Never criticize or talk about someone in a harmful, negative way.

• Never touch something that belongs to someone else without permission.

• Respect the privacy of every person, making sure to never intrude upon someone's quiet moments or personal space.

• Never interfere in the affairs of another by asking questions or offering advice.

• Never interrupt others.

• In another person's home, follow his or her customs rather than your own.

• Treat with respect all things held sacred to others whether you understand these things or not.

• Treat Earth as your mother; give to her, protect her, honor her; show deep respect for those in the animal world, plant world, and mineral world.

8. Listen to guidance offered by all of your surroundings; expect this guidance to come in the form of prayer, dreams, quiet solitude, and in the words and deeds of wise Elders and friends.

9. Listen with your heart.

10. Learn from your experiences, and always be open to new ones.

11. Always remember that a smile is something sacred, to be shared.

12. Live each day as it comes.

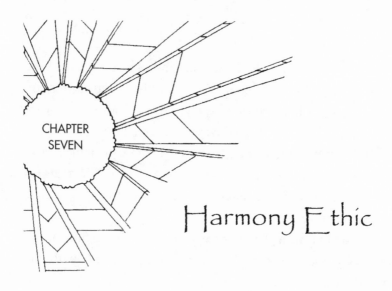

# Harmony Ethic

E very life is a very special gift from the Great One, and it is to be treated with gratitude and respect. Only with the help of all our relations may we truly live. The Wind gives our bodies our first breath and we carry its spirit with us wherever we go. Mother Earth provides us with food, a place to live, and anything else that we need. Water quenches our thirst, cleanses our bodies and our spirits, and gives of itself in all the ways that we ask. Grandfather Sun offers his warmth and his light so that all things may grow and flourish with life energy. All things are connected and exist in a continuing cycle of harmony and balance. However, it is important that we nurture this sacred flow of life energy, that we enhance it, that, at a minimum, we not disrupt it.

There is something known as the "Harmony Ethic," based on the communal spirit of cooperation and sharing, which guides much of traditional Cherokee living. It is a way of life that gives purpose and direction to much of our interaction in this world. In Cherokee tradition, wellness of the mind, body, spirit, and natural environment is an expression of the proper balance of all things. If we disturb or disrupt the natural balance of ourselves or others, illness may be the result, manifesting in the mind, body, spirit, or natural environment. However, all aspects are affected by such disturbances of the delicate balance as we easily realize when we abuse ourselves or others.

The Harmony Ethic is a way of maintaining the natural harmony and balance that exists within us, and with the world around us. It consists of:

**A nonaggressive and noncompetitive approach to life.** This is especially true if the goal of aggression or competition is individual success. If the goal of competition is to benefit the family, clan, tribe, or community, then competition is considered acceptable. Intertribal sports competitions, for example, can become quite aggressive. Competition or aggression for personal gain, however, is frowned upon.

**The use of intermediaries, or a neutral third person**, as a way of minimizing face-to-face hostility and disharmony in interpersonal relations. This involves the conscious avoidance of interpersonal conflict in an attempt to maintain reciprocally harmonious relations with "all one's relations." This is a common strategy in the traditional way for resolution of conflict without upsetting the natural balance of things.

**Reciprocity and the practice of generosity.** This occurs even when people cannot afford to be generous. It is the act of giving and of receiving that makes the Circle turn. Being able to share unselfishly frees a person to learn important lessons that are offered in life.

**A belief in immanent justice.** This relieves people from feeling the need to control others through direct interference, or to punish others. There is a natural order to things, and, sometimes, there are situations or experiences that are "out of our hands," so to speak. It is very important to be able to release something rather than harm ourselves or others with destructive emotions, thoughts, or actions. There is an old saying that we should never speak ill against another for the wind will carry it to that person, and eventually, the ill will return.

The Harmony Ethic is a system based upon caring for fellow human beings through the expression of deep respect and kindness. This is the way of a harmonious survival. It also emphasizes the presence of choice. To the Cherokee, a person has just as much choice in creating harmony as he or she does in creating disharmony and social disruption.

Life is very precious. Must we have something like a "close call" to realize this? Can we not recognize and embrace the beauty of all life without being splashed in the face by the Great One with a bucket of cold water?

Every life is, indeed, a precious gift to be respected and treated with care. This is not only out of respect for a gift that has been given, but also out of the belief that everything and everyone has a purpose to fulfill during his or her lifetime on Mother Earth. Every person, like every animal, tree, plant, and mineral, possesses some unique quality or talent to be discovered through a variety of experiences in this world. Harmony is the key to meaningful life experiences in which all learning contributes to an overall sense of our life purpose, and to harmony and balance. This purpose is mani-

fested by a striving for the wisdom and generosity exempli-
fied by the Elder who has accumulated a lifetime's worth of
experience in the world, and returned once again to the
child's first smile. Our Elders have spent much time on
Mother Earth, and they have seen much. Many have learned
the inner secrets to a harmonious way of life and they are the
keepers of this wisdom.

Traditional teachings relate to us how important it is
that we move through our lives with courage, humility,
respect, and kindness in our heart. All these things signify a
deep respect for the gift that we have been given in the breath
of life, as well as a respect for all life. Wisdom transcends all
circumstance, and ultimately comes from a harmony within
the self, and between the self and the universe—an inner
strength derived from the unity of spirit, natural environment, body, and mind. As Douglas Spotted Eagle says, "An
Elder once told me that I should always remember: 'All that
moves is sacred, only by understanding this can you realize
the rhythm of the Earth, and thereby know how to place your
feet'."

# The Principle of Noninterference

All things are alive, and all possess intrinsic worth. Native American spirituality focuses on the harmony and balance that come from our connection with all parts of the universe in which everything has the purpose and value exemplary of "personhood," including all plants (e.g., "tree people"), animals ("our four-legged brothers and sisters"), rocks and minerals ("rock people"), the land ("Mother Earth"), the winds ("the Four Powers"), "Father Sky," "Grandfather Sun," "Grandmother Moon," and "The Red Thunder Beings." As with humankind, all of these beings possess intrinsic worth and natural purpose in the greater scheme of things. Within this view lies the most powerful sense of belonging and connectedness, as well as a deep respect for "all our relations." Spiritual "being" essentially requires only that we seek our place in the universe; everything else will follow in good time. Since everyone and everything was created with a specific purpose to fulfill, no one should have the power to interfere or to impose upon others which is the best path to follow. This is the value of choice.

In the Medicine Way, the significance of relationship lies in a balance struck between an all-encompassing sense of belonging and connectedness with our relations and the practice of noninterference. The highest form of respect for another person is respecting his or her natural right to be self-determining. This means not interfering with another person's ability to choose, even when it is to keep that person from doing something foolish or dangerous. Every experience holds a valuable lesson—even in death, there is valuable learning that the spirit carries forth. Noninterference means caring in a respectful way. And it is the way of "right relationship."

Interfering with the activity of others, by way of aggression, for example, cannot and should not be encouraged or tolerated. This is not only disrespectful, but it violates the natural order of harmony and balance in which each being has to learn and experience life in his or her own way. Each person, each living being on Mother Earth, has his or her own Medicine that should not be disrupted or changed without that person choosing it. This is part of the learning. What moves the Circle is choice, and what keeps the Circle is kindness and respect for the natural flow of life-energy.

Jimm Good Tracks has said that "patience is the number one virtue governing Indian relationships." Respect often requires patience—demands patience—of us since things are rarely going to go the way that we expect them to. Yet, we have the tendency to want to change *how things are*, rather than changing *what we expect*. "Pain" is really nothing more than the difference between *what is* and *what we want it to be*. To be respectful of all things, we often must sacrifice expectation. This is the real beauty of noninterference. It gives us the ability to release some of the things that would otherwise bind us or weigh us down and disrupt our own natural flow. Indeed, some things really are "out of our hands," or at least we should approach them that way. Why take on the burden of something that would be better left alone or to run its own course, especially when it involves the choices of others? What others choose is not something we can control, nor should we attempt to do so. It is harmful both ways. Besides, what others choose is none of our business, and we should never assume that it is. This shows lack of wisdom and respect. It also shows a lack of trust in others' ability to choose, to experience, to learn.

You might be thinking, "Well, what if what they are choosing affects me?" This is a very valid and wise question. And truly, in the Circle, what others choose affects us all. We can only hope that they are walking the path of Good Medicine, and we can do what we must to protect ourselves if they are not. But it is never our place to change or influence them or their energy—unless we have permission from them. Even then, they still possess choice. Permission is very, very important. Think of how many times someone has entered "your space" without bothering to ask permission. How did that make you feel? How do others feel when you do the same to them. Is it any different? Is it necessary?

Think about the word "respect." What does it mean? What does it really mean? Well, it can mean many different things. But the word itself refers to the idea of "looking again" taken from the Latin ("re-" back + "specere" to look). What it implies is an openness and willingness to take a good look with deferential regard, or to view something or someone with great interest and admiration.

So why is respect so important? In order to answer that question, I will ask you by contrast to think back on some of the times when others have not bothered showing respect for you or the things that are important to you. Rather than asking if you now know the answer, I will ask if you *feel* the answer. Those times that you recalled were times in which your harmony and balance were disrupted, were they not? So why is respect so important? It is an honoring of the intrinsic worth possessed by every living being in the Greater Circle where nothing is greater or lesser than anything else. "All things are connected like the blood that unites one family."

Very often we think of respect in terms of something tangible that others must give to us when we have power over them in some way. We think not in terms of "relation," but in terms of "domination" and thus, "expectation." And so, even without thinking about it, we strive for power over others in some rather clever ways. That's real respect, right? Wrong.

All of us have our own personal distance, or our own "sacred space" that is controlled only by us, and filled only by us unless we invite someone else into it. And every one of us has, at one time or another, experienced a violation of our sacred space whether it was intentional or not. For example, someone bumps into us or stands too close. There are obvious social and cultural norms for what is considered appropriate distancing between people. However, there are many circumstances under which people have little choice over distancing as others violate our sacred space, either knowingly or unknowingly. We all know that feeling of awkwardness, of tension, of irritation, or outright anger and hostility. How dare they be so presumptuous and inconsiderate, right?

Sacred space is more than just physical space. It consists of all Four Directions, in the realm of mind, body, spirit, and natural environment. Just as we have all had the experience of someone bumping into us and not saying that they were sorry, we have all had the experience of someone telling us what to do, or pressuring us, or criticizing us, or manipulating us, and not giving us the choice or the chance. All these things take away choice, disrespect choice, and show little sign of "regarding with interest, deference, and admiration." And we have done the same to others as well. No one likes to be controlled. People are not meant to be controlled. No one wants to feel as though a choice is being violated. It does not feel good. Such things as asking intrusive questions, interrupting, speaking for others, telling others what to do, arguing, blaming, using sarcasm, sulking, being condescending, nitpicking, or using threats (both spoken and unspoken), are all fairly common occurrences. And we wonder why we may not feel well so much of the time? It is because we are violating the natural laws of Creation. It does not matter why we do it, what matters are the consequences of such actions that result in disharmony and discord.

Now, think about the word "expect." Literally, it means "looking out" from the Latin ("ex-" out + "spectare" to look at). Many times we interfere with others and others interfere with us simply because we have all done so without looking or by only looking out and never looking within. In some cases, we are not aware of what we do not see. In other cases, we are aware, but simply ignore what we see in favor of achieving whatever goal we have set for ourselves or others. And very often, we don't really need to achieve that goal as much as we think we do, or if we do need to achieve it, there is an appropriate way of going about it so as not to disrupt the natural flow of energies in harmony and balance. This is where the Harmony Ethic really comes in handy, for instance.

Noninterference stresses the importance of always asking permission, and not making unnecessary assumptions about others. It reminds us to always be thankful for what we have and not "expect" more than that, but rather to show "respect" for what we do have, and for the Greater Circle of which we are all a part. Think about the words "need to," "have to," "should." These words never cross your lips, right? Think about how often you use these words with others or yourself. Now and in the future, try a little experiment by attempting not to use these words on others or yourself. Eliminate them from your vocabulary if you can. Catch yourself as you think them. Try to catch yourself before the words leave your mouth, and think about what it is that you are saying or doing, and whether or not it is with respect . . . or expectation. Replace "need to," "have to," "should" with words like "want to," "choose to," "would like to" and see how it changes your life, your very way of thinking.

Above all, "respect" for others through patience, openness, and flexibility ultimately shows respect for yourself and your community. It is not uncommon in the traditional way for the withdrawal of a person during times of crisis to be allowed without question by the group, and without expectation. In addition, that person is to be welcomed back into the group without a required explanation for his or her absence. There is no need to interfere by asking what is wrong or offering solutions. Respect for another dictates that when a person is ready to share information, he or she will do so. Likewise, if a person is in need of assistance or advice, he or she will ask.

Virtue is a patience. Noninterference shows us that caring and respect are not one-in-the-same, but that both are required for harmonious relations. One of the highest forms of caring for another person comes through the expression of respect, that is, respecting a person's right and ability to choose, and practicing the patience to allow this person to do just that. This respect could be as simple as asking permission before touching someone.

We all help to create ourselves and experience our own Medicine through choices that are made. Every person deserves the opportunity and respect to make his or her own choices. There are lessons to be learned through the making of choices, and certain truths to be experienced through respect for the autonomy and presence of all living things.

The same philosophy applies to our relation with nature in which permission must be asked before taking, and thanks must be expressed by giving back in some way. This could be as simple as a small prayer giving thanks. It might mean sprinkling a little tobacco as an offering of gratitude for whatever has been received. It is not too much to ask, yet it makes a world of difference, and a real difference in our world.

# Keepers of the Wisdom

Our Elders, the "keepers of the wisdom," are considered highly respected persons due to the lifetime's worth of wisdom they have acquired through experience. Native American Elders have always played an important part in the continuance of the tribal community by functioning in the roles of parent, teacher, community leader, and spiritual guide. To refer to an Elder as Grandmother, Grandfather, Uncle, or Aunt, is to refer to a very special relationship that exists with that Elder through deep respect and admiration. To use these terms and other more general terms such as "old woman" or "old man" is to greatly honor someone who has achieved the status of Elder.

In the traditional way, Elders direct young children's attention outward to the things with which they co-exist (trees, plants, rocks, animals, elements, the land) and to the meaning of these things. They show the children the true relationship that exists with all things, and the way in which to honor this relationship. In this way, children develop a heightened level of sensitivity for everything of which they are a part and which is a part of them, for the circular (cyclical) motion and flow of life energy, and for the customs and traditions of their people.

There is a very special kind of relationship based on mutual respect and caring between Native American Elders and children as one moves through the Circle of Life from "being cared for" to "caring for," as John Red Horse puts it. With increase in age comes an increase in the sacred obligation to family, clan, and tribe. Native American Elders pass down to the children the tradition that their life force carries the spirits of their ancestors. With such an emphasis on connectedness, children are held in great reverence, not only as ones who will carry on the wisdom and traditions, but also as "little people" who are still very close to the spirit world and from whom we have much to learn. Larry Brendtro, Martin Brokenleg, and Steve Van Bockern relate a story shared with them by Eddie Belleroe, a Cree Elder from Alberta, Canada:

In a conversation with his aging grandfather, a young Indian man asked, "Grandfather, what is the purpose of life?" After a long time in thought, the old man looked up and said, "Grandson, children are the purpose of life. We were once children and someone cared for us, and now it is our time to care."

The power of caring and relation is immeasurable. Relationship focuses on a sense of connectedness, thankfulness, and the importance of giving back. Our Elders are the keepers of the sacred ways, as protectors, mentors, teachers, and support-givers, regardless of their "social status."

As we move from being a child to being an Elder, we can learn to listen to the spirit of a person, and to respect everyone for their intrinsic worth and being. And as we begin "caring for," we are reminded of the spirit of playfulness, innocence, and curiosity through the realization that there is always something to learn and always something to appreciate.

••••••••••••••••••••••••••••••••••••••••••••••••••••••••

## HUMILITY

We are important and unique as individuals, but we are also part of the Greater Circle of Life. As we come to view ourselves in relation to the Greater Circle, we begin to view our actions or intentions in terms of how they affect the Circle, whether it be the family, clan, tribe, community, or universe. One of our greatest challenges in life is to recognize our place in the universe and to honor this always.

Humility is essential to a harmonious way of life where the emphasis is placed upon relation rather than domination. Individual praise should be welcomed if it has been earned, but this praise need not be used to bolster a person in thinking or acting as though he or she is greater than any other living thing in the Circle. Boasting of accomplishments and loud behavior that attracts attention to the self are discouraged in the traditional way, where self-absorption and self-importance bring disharmony upon the self and the family.

In the Circle, the group must take precedence over the individual, and the wisdom of age takes precedence over youth, though it does not make anyone better or more worthy than anyone else. Many times, a traditional Native

American person will drop his or her head and eyes, or at least be careful not to look into the eyes of another, as a sign of respect for any Elder or other honored person. No one is worthy of staring into the eyes of an Elder, or looking into the spirit of that honored person. This is also an act that signifies that a person does not view him- or herself as better than anyone else.

.......................................................

## PATIENCE

Everything has its place. Very often, it is simply a matter of time before we recognize where and how things fit together. There is a sacred design to the world in which we live, to the process of life itself. And very often, it is not a matter of whether or not "things" fall into place, but whether or not our capacity for awareness and understanding of "things" falls into place.

It is important to be able to learn through careful observation, listening, and patience, as well as by asking questions or thinking things through. Everything offers us a valuable lesson, from all of our surroundings to each of our experiences. It takes time and a special kind of willingness or openness to receive all of the lessons that are offered to us throughout life.

.......................................................

## TIME

Life offers us opportunities to think in terms of what is happening now, and to be aware of what is taking place all around us, by focusing on current thoughts, ideas, feelings, and experiences. Where you are *is* where you have come from and where you are going. We do not always have to live by the clock. Mother Earth has her own unique rhythms that signal the beginnings and endings of things. Again, we need only to observe and listen quietly to know when it is time. So-called "Indian time" says that things begin when they are ready, and things end when they are finished.

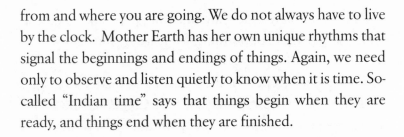

## BEING

The Medicine Way emphasizes a unique sense of "being" that allows us to live in accord with the natural flow of life energy. Being says, "It's enough just to be; our purpose in life is to develop the inner self in relation to everything around us." Being receives much of its power from connectedness. Belonging and connectedness lie at the very heart of where we came from, who we are, and to whom we belong. True "being" requires that we know and experience our connections, and that we honor our relations with all our heart.

## SHARING IS THE BEST MEDICINE

We always have much to learn and much for which to be thankful. Elders from all cultures are very special people and should be treated as such. They are the keepers of the wisdom, and they are the ones who have walked the path. And that is the best part about becoming an Elder. It is not that you know everything, because even Elders know that they are only beginning to learn. Besides, "When you think you know everything is when you don't know anything," as one Elder put it. Becoming an Elder means having something to share. It doesn't matter how big or small, everyone has something to share. But many Elders are in a unique position because they have had more opportunity for learning the right way to share it.

We are all keepers of the wisdom, no matter what age. Within each of us dwells the spirit of Creation. And as we move through the Circle of Life, we always have much to look forward to, knowing that the Circle flows through us with great strength and beauty. And all we have to do is open ourselves to its eternal movements.

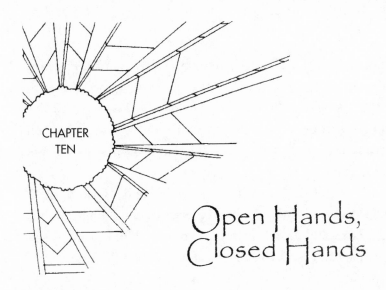

# Open Hands, Closed Hands

In the Cherokee traditional way, when children argued over an object, it was taken away from them and they were then encouraged to lie down on Mother Earth and look up at the sky. While observing the sky, the children were reminded that focusing attention on an object and on wanting to possess that object removed them from the harmony and balance of the Greater Circle. Then, the children were asked to focus their attention on Father Sky. "Look at the sky. Can you see the clouds? Watch the way they move and change before your eyes. Can you see images in the clouds? Can you see the spirit people there?"

The focus of the children's attention with possessing something was replaced with the openness of the sky and the movement of all our relations in the Above World, such as the clouds, the wind, the birds. "Should we seek to own the sky?" they might ask. Presence of mind was strengthened in the children as they opened their minds and hearts to the movement and language of the clouds who speak in shapes and pictures. The children might be asked to help out with a particular task as a way of replacing wanting thoughts with giving thoughts. This was only one of many ways in which to encourage openness, creativity, and humility in the face of all creation.

Try this, if you will: Close your hands. Clench them really tight. Tighter. Tighter. Clench them as tight as you can. Now, hold them as long as you can. Hold them. When you just can't hold your hands closed tight any longer, open them up.

How long did you last? It wasn't easy was it? Keep them open for several moments, then close them up again, and hold them real tight for as long as you can. Pay careful attention to how it feels. Feel the tightness. Watch your blood vessels pop out, and your knuckles turn white. When you just can't hold them anymore, open them up and let them loose.

Did you notice a difference (no, seriously)? Did you feel a difference between keeping them closed tight, and letting them open up? After awhile, holding your hands closed real tight doesn't feel very good. As a matter of fact, it starts to feel sort of bad, and may even hurt. It takes a lot more energy to keep your hands closed tight. And it feels relieving to just open them up and keep them loose.

Now, with your hands open, hold them so that your palms are facing upward. Remember what your hands looked like when you had them closed? That's right. Fists. And what we usually do with fists is send something, a "jaw-jacker" perhaps. Pay attention to the way your hands look now that they are open and ready to receive.

This is a lesson in "opening up" to the universe, and being open to receiving as well as sending. When our hands are open with palms up, we appear ready to receive, whether it be a gift, or a hug from someone special, or the soft tickling of raindrops, or the Sun's warmth.

When a baby smiles for the first time, that child has begun to open up to the universe in the ever-expanding awareness that he or she is alive, and to an ever-increasing "presence of mind" that need not fade as we grow older, but rather, flourish. How often do you find yourself stressed out because you're so busy or have so much on your mind that you just plain forget to smile. You may instead find that your forehead is furrowed and tight, that your shoulders and neck are tight, that your stomach is upset, that your heart races, or that your breathing is shallow, among many other things. This is the way of clenched fists. It stifles presence of mind. It suffocates the spirit and disrupts the harmony and balance.

A person can only hold his or her breath for so long before passing out. And when you're holding your breath, it is not a feeling of calm and clarity, but rather a feeling of tension and restlessness as you begin to black out. "Blacking out" metaphorically represents the onset of illness in any of the four realms—mind, body, spirit, natural environment. Because life is unpredictable and filled with challenges in all Four Directions, we cannot help but "hold our breath" from time to time as we face the challenges that life sends our way. "Holding our breath" is a natural means of protection and defense. But to live in a constant state of "breath-holding" is unwise.

They say that it takes more muscles to frown than to smile. The important point here is that it takes more *energy*

to frown than to smile . . . a lot more! And it is not free-flow-
ing energy as with the child's first smile, but choppy, disrupted energy emanating from us and returning to us as
restless rippling on the lake of our consciousness.

It takes a lot of energy to live a choppy way of life and to
keep ourselves closed up tight like clenched fists. And just
like clenched fists, we are always ready to fight or defend ourselves. Clenched fists make us tired, impatient, tense, and
even sick. We can only hold clenched fists for so long. We
can only hold our breath for so long. It takes real courage to
open ourselves up to the things around us, to notice things
we haven't noticed before, to experience things that we
wouldn't experience otherwise. All this means taking some
risks. That doesn't mean just opening up completely and letting everything come rushing in. What it means is being able
to open up when we want to and doing so without fear or
regret. This is essential for learning and growth as we allow
the Circle to move through us.

It is important to point out that "opening up" as used
here does not mean spilling your guts in search of catharsis
and resolution to some type of dysfunction or unfinished
business ("unresolved issues" as they would say in the mental
health arena). The process of opening-up refers here to the
reciprocal relations that occur within the Circle of Life in
which we are both giving and receiving in a respectful manner, and thereby strengthening and deepening our presence
of mind. Catharsis is the idea of transitioning by really stir-
ring things up. Opening-up is the idea of "settling" or seeking
a place of calm in the Circle through harmony and balance.
This is important for healing, but it is also important for simply living, learning, and growing.

One day, a long time ago, my father was up in the Great Smoky Mountains with his grandfather, learning some of the "ways" from the old man. They had walked way up into the mountains where they could gather certain herbs and other special things that can only be found in sacred places that are closer to Galun'lati, the Sky World. Grandfather was instructing my father to collect certain things as they went, and to carry everything that they had found. But this became increasingly more difficult as he only had so many pockets or other places in which to carry things, and it became more and more difficult to walk with so much stuff. But the old man was walking along easily, and he just kept finding more things for them to carry back. Pretty soon, my father's hands and arms were full, and all his pockets, too. He was completely loaded down with all these things, and had nowhere else to put anything. But Grandfather just kept on going. Suddenly, the old man spotted a very special stone that was rather large. He asked my father to pick it up, telling him that it was very, very important, and then he kept on walking. But my father, who could not pick up the special stone, answered in frustration, "But, Grandfather, my hands are full." The old man spun around and smiled cleverly. "Then I guess you'll just have to drop something," he said, and kept on going.

Our Native American Elders have taught us that we must remember where we stand in relation to everything else in order to know *where we are* and *who we are*. The goal then is continuity of mind, body, spirit, and natural environment—to exist in harmony and balance with the natural flow of all our relations. This is to walk in step with the universe. In order to do that, we must be open to the Greater Circle, recognizing with humility and respect where we stand in relation to everything else. This requires patience, openness, wisdom, and oftentimes, it means "letting go" in some way. This is not easy. Remember the image of clenched fists? They do not receive, they cannot . . . until they open up.

Now consider Squirrel Medicine and the many lessons offered by our little brother. Squirrel is the spirit of gathering and teaches us the importance of planning ahead for the winter when the trees will be bare and all the nuts will be long gone. He teaches us to always be prepared, and to always have plenty to share with others if need be. He teaches us the way of burying a special seed now, and watching it grow into the beautiful tree that will protect others in the future. He also offers us another lesson as well, and that is to not gather too many things so it becomes cumbersome, impractical, or harmful. Sometimes, it is important for us to lighten our load if we have gathered too many things that do not meet our needs, such as destructive thoughts, worries, pressures, stresses, or relationships that are hurtful. As Squirrel knows, there is a certain balance that must be struck in the process of gathering, in which one is prepared and fulfilled, but not overloaded or overwhelmed.

Squirrel scurries up the tree to a special hollow where he stores all of his goodies. This special place is an untroubled heart and mind in which to store the right amounts of wisdom and caring. Sometimes, opening-up to the universe requires that we let go of the things which weigh us down and disrupt our movement. Sometimes, if our hands are closed, or if they are completely full, we have to choose to drop something in order to open them up. And other times, we just have to open our hands in order to receive what the Circle has to give.

The process of living always involves something to learn, something to experience, something to understand. There are both "good" experiences and "bad" ones, depending on individual interpretation. There are people around us who are helpful, and there are those who are harmful to us. What we take away from each experience varies from situation to situation, time to time, and is simply a matter of perspective and choice. Unfortunately, we sometimes get so caught up in troubling experiences and the destructive thoughts and feelings that we are unable to experience the fulfilling ones. In a sense, we do not allow ourselves to experience the good experiences and to open up until we are ready, until we decide that whatever burden we are carrying is no longer worth carrying.

I sometimes use what I call the "River Rock Technique," and I will ask that you try it. First of all, think about all of your problems. Go through them in your mind and be as specific as you can (you may even want to make a list). Next, go down to the river, or whatever you have available to you, and choose one river rock for each of your problems. (Depending on what is available to you, you can substitute other kinds of rocks.) Ask permission of the rocks to join you for a period of time, inform them of your purpose, and offer thanks for their help. Choose the size and weight of each rock corresponding to the magnitude of each problem and ask the rocks for their permission to give the problem over to them. You may even want to choose a rock that just seems like that problem, maybe the way it looks, for instance. Remind yourself that healing is a very serious process and, therefore, the task at hand should be taken very seriously. After you have carefully and appropriately chosen your rocks, you must carry the river rocks you have chosen, keeping them with you at all times, even while sleeping. Remember to take this very seriously, just as we take life very seriously. Carry the rocks with you until you decide that you no longer wish to carry them, remembering that the rocks represent "problems" and cannot just be put down until there is "good" reason for doing so. This is a healing process and a very important lesson in choice. Once we have mastered Squirrel Medicine and the balance between gathering and letting go, then it is time to move on. As Snake would remind us, if your skin gets too tight, slide out of it.

The next important step in the opening-up process is to teach ourselves to experience not only through the mind, but also through the senses. Opening-up to the universe means really "feeling" life as it happens within you and all around you. Stillness is a pleasure as we learn to listen, observe, and enjoy the beauty around us with a sense of joy and great humility. This creates presence of mind through intuition, awareness, and a healing sense of calm.

Everything has energy. Our senses were designed so that we could perceive this energy in every living thing. All we have to do is teach ourselves how to listen to these things. We can see commonality just as easily as we can see difference; we can see beauty just as easily as we can see ugliness, and it is simply up to us which one we pay attention to. If you watch young children explore everything with all of their senses, you see the fascination in their eyes and the joy of discovery. We, too, have the capacity for this childlike fascination with every aroma, every texture, every sound, every taste, every color, shape, and movement. The world is very rich in beauty. Open up to all of your senses and explore the feelings that come to you. Touch things around you, feel them, listen to them, and really look at them, being sure to ask permission and give thanks. Experience the sense of joy, relaxation, and wonder. If you are not sure where to start, just take a young child out to spend some time with Mother Earth and let that child share his or her natural wisdom with you. You won't regret it!

When you are receiving in reciprocal fashion, it is only natural to continue the Circle by giving in turn. Think of someone who has helped you out in some way, especially when you really needed it. Where would you be right now if they had not helped you? "Opening-up" means being able to share as well as receive, and to do so in new and creative ways. That is the way of the Circle. And it is important to give to those who appreciate what you offer, and let go of those who do not.

Here's a good rule of thumb: For every person that helps you, it is your willing obligation to help seven others in turn. And they, too, must help seven others, and so on and so forth. In this way, the Circle of Life turns with the spirit of generosity and kindness. That is the way of the Circle.

The final thing to remember about opening-up is that a smile is something sacred and should be shared whenever possible. It is important to remember that even if we have nothing else to give, we always have a smile. And that is worth more than all the riches in the world.

"When a child smiles for the first time . . ."

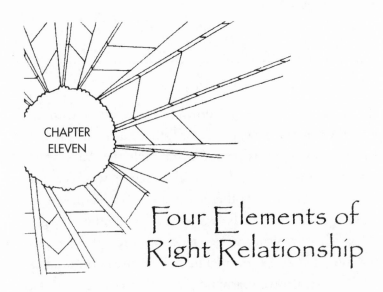

CHAPTER
ELEVEN

# Four Elements of Right Relationship

## ACKNOWLEDGMENT

Each day, with the rising of the Sun, we are again bathed in its warmth and light. As the night sky fades into the west, and the Sun renews its path along the great skyvault, we are again reminded of the Circle, ongoing, everlasting. The young flowers bend themselves toward the brightness and open their petals to receive its life-energy. In the traditional way, we greet the Sun every morning, giving thanks. Every day, we acknowledge Grandfather Sun's warmth and light as everything on Mother Earth grows strong and flourishes in its beauty. Grandfather Sun is sacred and so, too, are his children, the Fire. Every day, we can acknowledge the beauty in every living thing by taking the time to notice it. The same is true of our relations with other people. We should acknowledge the warmth and light in everyone. We can acknowledge the sacred fire in every living thing. We all share much in common no matter who we are or where we come from. We are all part of the same family.

........................................................

## ATTENTION

One day, my father was down by the riverside with his grandfather, learning the ways of Mother Earth and all that she teaches us. He was observing carefully the Ways being taught to him by his grandfather, although he was feeling a little overwhelmed since there is so much to learn, just as Mother Earth has so much to offer us. Grandfather was giving thanks to the water when, suddenly, my father said to him, "Grandfather, I know that these Ways are good and this is well . . . but if I went around giving thanks to everything that there is all the time, I would never get anything done." The wise old man smiled as he continued and said, "That's right."

Mother Earth has been around since the beginning of time. She has undergone many changes and she has endured with great splendor and mystery. We little spirits have been around for a long time too. And we have only survived because of the attention that Mother Earth has devoted to us, her children, providing us with all the things that we need to live and grow. We too must give our attention to Mother Earth as she requires nurturing and care. Try to find time every once in awhile to just go out and spend some time with Mother Earth, even if it's for only fifteen minutes.

People also need attention through caring and time for sharing. Think about all the special people in your life. When was the last time you just picked up the phone and called an old friend, or spent some time together with someone you love, not "doing" anything in particular, but just "being?" Why not take that special person with you to spend some time with Mother Earth, maybe having a picnic, or going for a swim in the lake, or just going for a nice quiet walk together. And as always, give thanks for the beauty and for anything that you receive.

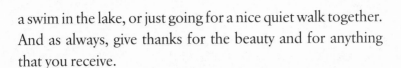

## APPRECIATION

Imagine the sound of raindrops falling on leaves, gently, steadily. Can you hear that soothing sound in your mind? Can you almost feel it in your heart? It is soothing, isn't it?

Now picture yourself looking at the still surface of a pond or a lake. You can, at once, see both your reflection in the surface and the depths of what lies beneath.

Imagine the sound of a mountain river rushing over heavy rocks, and the feel of a soft mist on your face from the river's steady motion. Can you hear the river singing its song?

Water is purifying and healing in its gentleness and its enormous strength. Water quenches our thirst. It cleanses our body, mind, and spirit of toxins, and gives of itself in all ways so that we may live. As we grew inside our mothers, we were surrounded by the comfort of Water. The spirit of Water is that of purity, and it reminds us of the importance of appreciating and embracing the natural flow. It reminds us that we, too, are liquid beings (our bodies are some 80 percent water) who must flow in order to be in our best Medicine. Water is one of the most powerful elements because of its ability to absorb such enormous amounts of energy. We, too, have the ability to embrace the energy of all things and to value the energy that makes every living thing unique.

......................................................

## AFFECTION

When we are born, Wind gives us our first breath. From that time on, Wind is always with us as we inhale and exhale, inhale and exhale. We are, during our time on Mother Earth, forever receiving and giving back. So, too, Wind enters our bodies, our minds, our spirits, bringing solitude and strength, and leaves us, taking uncertainty and fear with it to transform this disharmony into gentle energy. Every breath is a prayer offered to the Wind. Right now, inhale as you count to "4," then slowly exhale, counting backward from "7." Do this four times, and give thanks each time. Do you feel a difference?

The spirit of Wind is that of calm and quiet. Wind is most generous in its movement. Wind breathes life upon all things, and carries away destructive energies, replacing them with a sense of calm. Just as Wind breathes life into us, we have the ability to breathe life into those around us by acting upon our caring for others.

When you get a chance, why not do something special to show affection for Mother Earth and all our relations? For instance, plant a tree. Or put some birdseed out for our winged brothers and sisters. Just do whatever feels right to you as you express your appreciation for all those things that are important to you. Do something special to show your appreciation for the special people in your life. Plant a good feeling in them and watch it grow. Tell them something that you like about them. Tell them that they look nice. Anything. Breathe life into other living things, and watch that life energy return to you in the eternal movement of the Greater Circle of Life.

# Between Hawk and Eagle

Opening up to all our relations includes learning the importance of observing and listening to lessons offered by our brothers and sisters of the animal world. Therein lies powerful Medicine that may guide all of us on our life-journey. One such lesson comes from considering the difference between Hawk and Eagle. Paula Underwood Spencer, an Oneida, describes this difference between our two powerful winged brothers:

> When hunting, Hawk sees Mouse . . . and dives directly for it.
> When hunting, Eagle sees the whole pattern . . . sees movement in the general pattern . . . and dives for the movement, learning only later that it is Mouse.

Observing the difference between Hawk and Eagle teaches us the difference between Specificity and Wholeness. All things are connected, and all things are constantly in motion, just as the energy of life is constantly moving and changing. Wholeness shows us the motion of all things, and

Specificity gives us a point of reference from which to view all things by reminding us of "relation" or relationship between one thing and another.

Through Eagle, we are reminded of the great expanse of the universe and its circular motion of interconnectedness and interdependence, remembering always to keep the larger picture in view as we move through life. Through Hawk, we are reminded of the need to remember where we are in relation to everything else, focusing neither completely on ourselves, nor on everything else, but rather, recognizing the relationship that exists and honoring that relationship at all times.

To be able to draw upon the power of our winged brothers and sisters is to draw upon the power of perspective in our relationship to all things. With the wisdom of the Elders, we seek to understand our place in the universe and what it is that we have to share. We seek to walk in step with the universe and its eternal rhythms. We seek to feel our relationship with Creation, and to contribute to the Greater Circle in whatever way we can. And as we develop our own inner vision, we are able to soar upon the wings of both Specificity and Wholeness, using our capacity for perspective to deepen clarity of thought and action in our lives. To soar upon the wings of both Hawk and Eagle, that is true presence of mind.

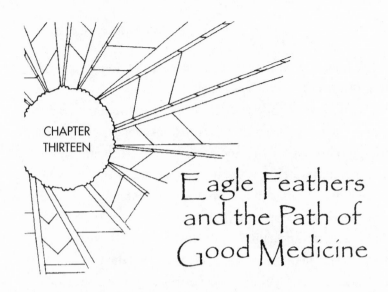

# Eagle Feathers and the Path of Good Medicine

*Eagle Medicine is the power of the Great Spirit,*
*the connection to the Divine. It is the ability to live*
*in the realm of spirit, and yet remain connected*
*and balanced within the realm of Earth. Eagle*
*soars, and is quick to observe expansiveness within*
*the overall pattern of life. From the heights of the*
*clouds, Eagle is close to the heavens where the*
*Great Spirit dwells.*

—JAMIE SAMS, SENECA/CHOCTAW, AND DAVID CARSON, CHOCTAW

Eagle feathers are considered infinitely sacred to traditional Native American people who make use of the feathers for a variety of purposes including ceremonial healing and purification. Eagle Medicine represents a state of presence achieved through diligence, understanding, awareness, and completion of "tests of initiation" such as the vision quest or other demanding life-experiences. Elder status is associated with Eagle Medicine and the power of connectedness and truth. It is through the wisdom of experience that this Medicine is earned.

The eagle feather, which represents duality, tells the story of life. It tells of the many dualities that exist in life, such as light and dark, male and female, substance and shadow, summer and winter, peace and war, life and death. It reminds us of the teachings that Opposites are extensions of themselves like two opposing hands of the same body. Native American traditionalists look upon the eagle feather as a sacred symbol of the balance necessary for the Circle of Life to continue. My father, J. T. Garrett, as a member of the Eastern Band of Cherokee, describes how:

> The eagle feather teaches us about the Rule of Opposites, about everything being divided into two ways. The more one is caught up in the physical, or the West, then the more one has to go in the opposite direction, the East, or the spiritual, to get balance. And it works the other way, too —you can't just focus on the spiritual to the exclusion of the physical. You need harmony in all Four Directions.

The lesson of Opposites is that of choice. Any two Opposites are often part of the same truth. If we consider the eagle feather with its light and dark colors, we could argue that "the dark colors are far more beautiful and, therefore, naturally more valuable," or vice versa. Regardless of which colors are said to be more beautiful, or necessary, or valuable, the truth is the bottom line: Both colors come from the same feather, both are true, they are connected, and it takes both to fly.

The balance of which the traditional way speaks is not a recognition of two separate phenomena, nor a decision as to which is best and which is worst. The balance of which the traditional way speaks is a recognition of the "oneness" of two differing phenomena, and a decision to honor both through harmony and balance. Traditionally, a person *earns* the eagle feather through enormous acts of courage, understanding, or generosity. Very often, it is through such acts that this recognition of "oneness" or truth occurs, and it is here that universal learning takes place.

# When Eagle Speaks

To walk in beauty is to celebrate the Sacred Dance of Life, to join the Circle with an open mind and an open heart, and to move at our own pace with clarity, kindness, and a sense of calm. To walk in beauty is to understand and practice the way of right relationship and to appreciate all of the beauty that exists both within and all around us.

Eagle asks, "Do you want to learn how to fly? Do you want to see great Creation through my eyes? Do you want to dance on the wind as I do?" The young boy and young girl dance, offering thanks for all things, walking in step with the universe and its eternal movements. The young boy and young girl dance. Within them, all around them, Creation dances in its sacred rhythm, and keeps on dancing.

When Eagle speaks, he speaks in the way that he moves. He speaks with his eyes, with his balance, with his presence. He speaks from the energy and power of the Four Directions, and their sacred flow. He speaks from the

"Galun'lati," the Above World, and from "A-lo-hi," Mother
Earth, the Center. He speaks from the truth that soars in his
heart and in his spirit. And as he speaks, he walks in beauty.
And so, it is good.

# Blessing Way

O Great One, I come before you in a humble manner, giving thanks for all living beings in Creation. I offer the clarity of my mind, body, spirit, and natural space in prayer to you, O Great One, for the spirit of all Creation. I offer great thanks and what gifts I have to the Four Sacred Directions and powers of the universe and I pray:

> To the spirit of Fire in the East,
> To the spirit of Earth in the South,
> To the spirit of Water in the West,
> To the spirit of Wind in the North.

I pray and give thanks to you, O Great One. I pray and give thanks to Mother Earth, Father Sky, Grandfather Sun, Grandmother Moon, and all our relations in the Greater Circle of Life. I thank you for your power, energy, wisdom, and sacred gifts, because without you and the guidance of all my relations, I would not be able to live, and love, and grow, and feel, and learn. I ask that I be shown another way if I have ever harmed or hurt other living things. I pray, offering what gifts I have, that you may guide us, heal us, purify us, and protect us. I pray for all our relations that we may exist together in harmony and balance. "Wah Doh."

# Bibliography

Bradley, R. K. *Weavers of Tales*. Cherokee, NC: Betty Dupree, 1967.

Brendtro, L. K., Brokenleg, M., & Van Bockern, S. *Reclaiming Youth at Risk: Our Hope for the Future.* Bloomington, IN: National Education Service, 1990.

Brown, V., & Johnson, P. *Return of the Indian Spirit.* Berkeley, CA: Celestial Arts, 1981.

Chief Seattle. *How Can One Sell the Air?: A Manifesto for the Earth.* Summertown, TN: Book Publishing Company, 1988.

DuBray, W. H. "American Indian Values: Critical Factor in Casework." *Social Casework,* 66, pp. 30–37, 1985.

Four Worlds Development Project. *The Sacred Tree: Reflections on Native American Spirituality.* Wilmot, WI: Lotus Light, 1984.

Garrett, J. T. "Where the Medicine Wheel Meets Medical Science." In S. McFadden (ed.), *Profiles in Wisdom: Native Elders Speak about the Earth* (pp. 167–179). Santa Fe, NM: Bear & Company, 1991.

Good Tracks, J. G. "Native American Noninterference." *Social Casework,* 18 (6), pp. 30–34, 1973.

Lake, M. G. *Native Healer: Initiation into an Ancient Art.* Wheaton, IL: Quest Books, 1991.

Locust, C. *American Indian Beliefs Concerning Health and Unwellness.* Native American Research and Training Center Monograph, University of Arizona, 1985.

Loftin, J. D. "The 'Harmony Ethic' of the Conservative Eastern Cherokees: A Religious Interpretation." *Journal of Cherokee Studies,* Spring, 1983.

Mooney, J. *Myths of the Cherokee and Sacred Formulas of the Cherokees.* Nashville, TN: Charles Elder, 1972.

Red Horse, J. G. "Indian Elders: Unifiers of Families." *Social Casework,* 61(8), pp. 490–493, 1980.

Sams, J. & Carson, D. *Medicine Cards: The Discovery of Power Through the Ways of Animals.* Santa Fe, NM: Bear & Company, 1988.

Spencer, P. U. "A Native American Worldview." *Noetic Sciences Review,* Summer, 1990, pp. 14–20.

Ywahoo, D. *Voices of Our Ancestors: Cherokee Teachings from the Wisdom Fire.* Boston: Shambhala, 1987.

# About the Authors

J. T. (Jasper Thomas) Garrett, Ed.D., a member of the Eastern Band of Cherokee Indians from North Carolina, has been a student and teacher of Indian Medicine for over thirty-five years. He and Michael teach a weekend gathering, entitled "Full Circle," utilizing Native American teachings and wisdom of the Elders to guide participants in seeking a path to harmony and balance. His career includes thirty years in hospital administration, environmental/occupational safety, and public health administration.

Michael Tlanusta Garrett, Ph.D., is an assistant professor of Counselor Education at the University of North Carolina at Charlotte. He has authored numerous articles with a unique perspective, professionally and personally, on Native American concerns. Michael has worked with children and adolescents in schools; has been a group therapist in community agency settings; and has taught several courses and seminars on cultural diversity. Michael grew up on the Cherokee Indian Reservation in western North Carolina.

# BOOKS OF RELATED INTEREST

WALKING ON THE WIND
Cherokee Teachings for Harmony and Balance
*by Michael Garrett*

MEDITATIONS WITH THE CHEROKEE
Prayers, Songs, and Stories of Healing and Harmony
*by J. T. Garrett*

THE CHEROKEE SACRED CALENDAR
A Handbook of the Ancient Native American Tradition
*by Raven Hail*

MASTERY OF AWARENESS
Living the Agreements
*by Doña Bernadette Vigil with Arlene Broska, Ph.D.*

THE WORLD IS AS YOU DREAM IT
Shamanic Teachings from the Amazon and Andes
*by John Perkins*

THE TOLTEC PATH OF RECAPITULATION
Healing Your Past to Free Your Soul
*by Victor Sanchez*

DANCE OF THE FOUR WINDS
Secrets of the Inca Medicine Wheel
*by Alberto Villoldo and Erik Jendresen*

ORIGINAL WISDOM
Stories of an Ancient Way of Knowing
*by Robert Wolff*

Inner Traditions • Bear & Company
P.O. Box 388
Rochester, VT 05767
1-800-246-8648
www.InnerTraditions.com

Or contact your local bookseller